Praise for *Cracked, Not Broken*

"Kevin's remarkable story of resilience and courage provides keen insight into the intense ambivalence experienced by those who struggle with thoughts of suicide. It is tragic to think about the hundreds who may have similarly wished like Kevin to be back on the bridge immediately after jumping. However, it is also extremely hopeful that lives can be saved even when someone is truly intent on ending their pain. *Cracked, Not Broken* proclaims, 'suicide is not inevitable for anyone' and that belief is strengthening commitment to suicide prevention everywhere from the Golden Gate Bridge to the U.S. health care system." —**David Covington**, Vice President, Adult & Youth Services, Magellan Health Services

"Kevin is an extraordinary person with an inspirational story. This book should be mandatory reading for all health, social care, educational, government, and front line professionals—in fact everyone! Kevin has an extremely powerful message of hope for all." —**Alys Cole-King**, FRC, Psych, consultant psychiatrist, Royal College of Psychiatrists spokesperson on suicide and self-harm, Connecting with People training co-founder, and medical director Open Minds Alliance CIC/United Kingdom

"Suicidal individuals often approach the edge of life and death, few catapult themselves over that edge and into the abyss below and return to talk about [it]. Kevin Hines knows. He has reflected, plummeting at 75 mph toward a freezing cold 'certain death' on 'what have I done?' and 'I want to live' while racing toward death. Hines gives us all hope, strength, and courage to face another day, take on the challenges of life, and keep 'living well.'" —**William Schmitz Jr.**, PsyD, president-elect, American Association of Suicidology

"A compelling look into the despair of mental illness and the fight for mental wellness" —**Brandy Mychals,** bestselling author of *How to Read a Client from Across the Room*

"Kevin Hines's memoir is a startling, hair-raising, and compulsively readable account of one man's descent into the hell of bipolar disorder. It is a courageous testament of a man facing the tragedy of mental illness. Every person suffering with mental illness (or family member or friend) should read this book as soon as possible because it will save lives." —**Andy Behrman**, author of *Electroboy: A Memoir of Mania*

"Kevin Hines's book is both mesmerizing and eye-opening. It sheds light on the impulse and momentum that lead to a suicide crisis in a gripping, heart-pounding story that should make a believer out of anyone who has wondered how suicides happen." —**Eve R. Meyer**, executive director, San Francisco Suicide Prevention

"This account of Hines's suicide attempt—and his blazing struggle back to wellness—is harrowing, honest, and deeply human shot through with his heartfelt insight and, often surprisingly, great sense of humor. The people in these pages, from Uncle Kevin to the fellow inmates of the wards, are drawn with precision and grace. Cracked, Not Broken shows us the darkness in great detail, but this book ultimately leads us to the light." —**Scott Hutchins**, author of A Working Theory of Love, editor's choice for the New York Times Sunday Book Review

"Kevin's journey will take you to the edge of despair and back. He has become an inspirational advocate for those suffering from mental illness since the day he took a fast and fateful leap off the Golden Gate Bridge in an attempt to end his life. His story will surely find a home in the hearts of many seeking guidance." —**Jennifer Storm**, executive director of the Victims/Witness Assistance Program, advocate and author of multiple books on trauma and recovery

"A story of faith, courage, luck, and persistence. It's an affirmation of life and how, if given a second chance, a person can move from the deepest depths of despair to a calling that helps save others from the precipice." —**John Bateson**, author of The Final Leap: Suicide on the Golden Gate Bridge

"Kevin Hines's memoir Cracked, Not Broken is both gut wrenching and heart-warming all at the same time. As I was reading it, I experienced the most extreme emotions, moved from laughter to tears countess times. Because our son was also named 'Kevin,' I imagined it all through his mind and soul; therefore this book has impacted me on a very personal level. Kevin Hines is a gifted speaker and writer but most importantly a beacon of light for anyone battling mental illness or loves someone who is. I could only hope that our 'Kevin' would have had this same courage had he survived his own suicide. Kevin Hines honestly shares his desperate struggle to survive in spite of life-threatening injuries, barriers to care, and gaps in our mental health system. He reminds us all that life is a precious gift that can only be lived one day at a time." —**Carol Graham,** wife of Major General, U.S. Army (Retired) who lost one son to suicide and one son to the war in Iraq

"In Cracked, Not Broken, Kevin captures the anguish and humanity of his struggles against the compelling voices in his head. Those voices drove Kevin to leap from the Golden Gate Bridge—a leap that should have killed him. Kevin writes with hard-earned insight and gripping candor about his terrible ambivalence about life and death leading to his jump. Believing he had run out of options, Kevin obeyed the commanding voices and hurdled the rail. Only as he hit free-fall did Kevin realize that he still had options to explore and a life to live. Kevin's survival is a gift to us all as he is able to write with rare insight gained from that horrific experience.

As in his public presentations, in this narrative Kevin Hines moves us with his story of mental torment, survival, and his ongoing recovery. Kevin brings tremendous courage as he publicly addresses his personal trials. He describes his mental illness and his reclaiming of his life from the perspective of one who has been given a second chance. His life-affirming story is not to be missed." —**Donn Marshall**, PhD associate dean of Students Director and Chief Psychologist, Counseling, Health & Wellness Services, University of Puget Sound, Washington

"Kevin Hines's story is an important one. Of the more than 1,600 suicides from the Golden Gate Bridge since its construction in 1937, fewer than thirty-five individuals have survived. Kevin reports that while falling toward the water, he realized how desperately he wanted to live. Other suicide survivors tell similar tales, impressing upon us how impulsive and thus preventable and treatable suicide is. Kevin's survival . . . is a blessing for us all." —**Mel Blaustein**, MD, medical director of psychiatry, St. Francis Hospital, San Francisco

"*Cracked, Not Broken* is an amazing and absorbing story about a man with a tremendous will to survive even when his own mind is telling him he must die. After years of speaking all over the world to encourage others and to prevent suicide, he has gifted us with a book describing the experience and thoughts affected by his mental illness in illuminating detail. His story inspires us to believe in the incredible ability of people to recover and grow stronger." —**Helynna Brooke**, executive director, San Francisco Mental Health Board

"One of my very first contacts in a psychiatric hospital was in 1965 with a woman who had been deeply depressed and who, like Kevin Hines, attempted suicide by jumping off of a bridge. Unfortunately, although she survived she was permanently disabled and unable to speak. I wish that I had been able to read *Cracked, Not Broken* at that time in order to gain a better understanding of what her experience might have been. This book may have served as a voice for her. Kevin Hines's work captures the ongoing nature of serious and persistent mental illness, but leavens it with humanity, hope, and understanding." —**Russell Lee**, licensed psychologist and emeritus professor of psychology, Bemidji State University

"Kevin shares a compelling, at times disturbing, but always remarkably helpful story of his journey from certain death to eventual rebirth and recovery. The raw intimacy of Kevin's story will help not only those struggling with mental illness and suicidality, but also professionals committed to helping guide recovery. I walked away having been moved, educated, and inspired. In the end, Kevin's story is one of simple truths, that there's no easy way through life, that struggles will come, and that the one essential to happiness and well-being are the relationships that make up the fabric of our lives. Every clinician and any person suffering from a mental illness (and anyone who loves them) should read Kevin's story and remind themselves daily that a caring, committed, and enduring relationship not only makes all the difference in the world, it saves lives." —**M. David Rudd**, PhD, ABPP, dean of the College of Social and Behavioral Science, University of Utah; former president of the American Association of Sucidology; cofounder and scientific director of the National Center for Veterans Studies

"*Cracked, Not Broken* offers a window into a personal struggle with mental illness, ranging from the joy of recovery to the despair of relapse. Kevin Hines's remarkable story is one of hope, balanced with the realities of living with mental illness one day at a time. It is an inspiration to those who strive to live well every day and to their concerned family members." —**Jeremy W. Pettit**, PhD, author of *The Interpersonal Solution to Depression* and over eighty-five publications on depression, anxiety, and suicide

"Many people will be drawn to Kevin Hines because of his tragic and near-fatal experience at the Golden Gate Bridge. Once engaged, they will find that his voice and story represent much more: a true tale of the complex life factors that can culminate in a suicide attempt; a revealing glimpse of the mental state of someone in the moments just before and during a suicide attempt; an inspirational model of recovery and thriving; and a seasoned perspective gained from sharing his experiences widely with all those concerned with suicide prevention. *Cracked, Not Broken* compellingly weaves together these strands." —**Thomas Joiner**, PhD; author of *Why People Die by Suicide*

"Kevin Hines is not 'cured,' he survives and thrives with chronic mental illness. From an almost always fatal suicide attempt through recovery and his emergence as an outspoken public figure and mental health advocate, Kevin tells us something every person with mental illness needs to hear—you too can survive and thrive." —**Paul Muller**, founding member, Bridge Rail Foundation

Cracked, Not Broken

Cracked, Not Broken

Surviving and Thriving
After a Suicide Attempt

Kevin Hines

ROWMAN & LITTLEFIELD PUBLISHERS, INC.
Lanham • Boulder • New York • Toronto • Plymouth, UK

Published by Rowman & Littlefield Publishers, Inc.
A wholly owned subsidiary of The Rowman & Littlefield Publishing Group, Inc.
4501 Forbes Boulevard, Suite 200, Lanham, Maryland 20706
www.rowman.com

10 Thornbury Road, Plymouth PL6 7PP, United Kingdom

British Library Cataloguing in Publication Information Available

Library of Congress Cataloging-in-Publication Data
Hines, Kevin, 1981–
    Cracked, not broken : surviving and thriving after a suicide attempt / Kevin Hines.
        pages cm
    Includes bibliographical references and index.
    ISBN 978-1-4422-2240-3 (cloth : alk. paper)—
    ISBN 978-1-4422-2241-0 (ebook)
        1. Kevin Hines, 1981–. 2. Mentally ill—United States—Biography. 3. Mental health services—United States. 4. Suicide—psychological aspects. I. Title.
    RC464.H56 A3 2013
    616.890092 B—dc23   2013009874

♾™ The paper used in this publication meets the minimum requirements of American National Standard for Information Sciences—Permanence of Paper for Printed Library Materials, ANSI/NISO Z39.48-1992.

Printed in the United States of America

My Rock, My Love, My Life…
Mrs. Hines

Yesterday is History
Tomorrow is a Mystery
Today is a Gift
That is Why They Call it the Present

—Babatunde Olatunji

Let us always and forever cherish today

—KH

He is ancient yet ageless
He is ticking yet timeless
He runs, not hunted, he chases
He is a man of many faces
He is the darkness
I am the light
I was Cracked . . . But will never be Broken

—*The Bipolar Mind*, KH

Contents

~

Foreword

DR. DANIEL J. REIDENBERG,
PSYD, FAPA, FACFEI, CRS, BCPC, CMT
EXECUTIVE DIRECTOR OF SAVE

The most powerful organ in the body can sometimes fail to work properly. It can lose its ability to function as designed: to keep us healthy, alive, safe; to allow us joys and fears, ecstasy and sorrow. The mind works autocratically, performing some functions without ever thinking about them (breathing, hunger, regulating sleep), to functions we want to do (play, read, learn, etc.). It is, in the end, our most incredibly powerful and awesome organ.

What happens, however, when the mind loses control? What happens when its chemicals are out of balance? What happens when electrical impulses and wires (nerves) cross? This is what happens to the brain of those living with mental illnesses (more accurately, "brain illnesses"). The brain does not function as it should; life is out of control. The brain alters our bodies; thoughts are distorted, emotions are unregulated, and behaviors we once thought could never occur happen. One of the most challenging, exhausting, and painful phenomena we do as humans is to live and survive with these changes in our minds. The toll it takes on an individual's body and the people in their lives is, tragically, often too much to bear.

Most of us have seen news stories about people who were "psychotic" or "mentally ill" when they allegedly or were found guilty of having done some horrible, heinous act. Each year people are murdered, raped,

robbed, tortured, and many other horrific acts are done by those suffering with the most tormented and troubled minds. Often after the
crimes have been committed, we hear the reports of people that say
they knew something was wrong, but they didn't know what and they
definitely had no idea that this would happen. They are telling the
truth because the logical, rational, normally functioning mind can't
envision some of the horrors that the mind of someone who is sick can.
It's almost impossible and quite honestly if they could; we ought to be
concerned about them as well.

Kevin Hines is a living, walking miracle. He is, by all accounts, the
antithesis of the person who lives with the psychotic mind. Rather
than hurt, he helps. If you have ever wondered exactly what it is like to
live inside of the mind of someone who has a mental illness but be far
enough from it that you aren't hurt by it, then Kevin's story is the one
you want to read. It is his mind that you want to get inside of.

In *Cracked, Not Broken: Surviving and Thriving After a Suicide Attempt*, Hines takes you on a journey from perfect wellness and happiness, to the depths of an emotional despair and isolation no one should
ever have to endure. Along the journey you get to experience, just as
he did, the neglect and abandonment by his biological parents to the
joy of being adopted into "a beautiful, melting pot of a family." Walk
with Kevin as he goes through school excelling at sports in high school.
Then, as his mind begins to lose control and contact with reality, keep
walking with him as he struggles to hold on to what is real.

While you journey with Hines, his family and friends, you will feel
the hope that they had when finding "the best" psychiatrist in San
Francisco. You will also feel the depths of the dark hours he spent hearing voices that were not his own telling him wild, fanciful delusions of
greatness, as well as his paranoid fears of being watched and haunted,
like when he thought he was being hunted down by men in white mail
trucks coming to get him.

It is the deepest, darkest of places that he takes you to that will hurt
the most and scare you; that a mind could go to that place while still
holding onto a tear of sadness rolling down his face as he says goodbye
to his father for what he believes will be the very last time. As Kevin
walks you through the last day, hours, and moments before his ultimate

act—following what his mind tells him to do in taking his own life—you will see that miracles can, and do happen.

Hines jumped from a place not made to do so. He attempted to end his pain by taking his life in a way so utterly unfathomable and painful most of us cannot comprehend it. Yet, for Hines, the moment, the very instant, the split second that his hands left that railing and his mind realized he was free-falling in mid-air, he didn't want to die. He prays, "Oh God, what have I done? I don't want to die! God please save me."

This quite possibly was the most real thought his mind had in the weeks leading up to that moment in September of the year 2000. But, as he is falling from hundreds of feet in the air on the way to an almost 100% chance of death, his mind was shocked back into reality; the reality that he was going to die in seconds. But he did not die, and this is his story. It is a story of recovery, relapse, further recovery and ultimately hope. He is Cracked...Not Broken, or he has learned the art of living mentally well and this is the Kevin Hines story.

~

Acknowledgments

First and foremost, my deepest love and gratitude goes to the steadfast rock in my life, my beautiful and loving wife, Mrs. Hines. Without her I would be lost. Next to life she is the greatest gift I have ever known. Thank you, Marcia Silvera and Martino Ferralis, for creating me. Thank you God for creating them. Thank you Patrick and Debra Hines for making me your son. You raised me right, with great passion, and unconditional love. I feel forever in your debt for all that you have shown me, taught me, and given me. To my siblings Joseph, Elizabeth, Jordache, Somesh, and Shikha I am grateful for your love and contributions to my growth and your aid in molding the vision of the path I walk today. To my aunts, uncles, cousins family and friends I value all of you and your guidance, constant care and love in my life. I will always be grateful for your presence.

John Fennell, you were a tremendous mentor. May you always rest in peace.

Mom, we had our difficult times. However the strength you instilled in me to keep on truckin' – to keep on keepin' on and to find positivity in the darkest of hours will always be cherished and never be forgotten. Thank you, Mom, for your optimism and love. Thank you Mom, for everything.

Dad, you stuck with me in the most painful of times. You never let go . . . . I am so grateful to have a strong man like you in my life. Like an angel on earth, you stayed by my side when I needed you most. I feel so blessed to have you as my father, I am so thankful; words cannot express the way I feel about you. You were a tough love kind of guy but deep down you always believed in what I could accomplish and what I would become. Dad, you were the best man at my wedding for a reason. I love you.

To Prima Cosa Café, thank you for letting me set up shop in your spot. It was my second home because of you guys and your 'Best Ever Vanilla Soy Café Latte,' I got this book done. I could not have done it without the caffeine and amazing service.

I have gone through a lot, but no one can deny that my life has been blessed.

A special thanks to Phyllis Parsons, Katie, Rebecca and John Drinkwater from the Parsons Company. If it wasn't for Phyllis Parsons and her gentle and bright affirmations, this book would not exist. Nor would the focus of my life's work be moving so fast in the right direction. Phyllis, you are a gem of a human being. I am so thankful. I am so grateful. Phyllis you are appreciated. You are loved.

To the band 'Friends of Emmet': I am thankful for knowing you and grateful for the enrichment you have brought to my life and demonstrating to me the true power of song. Your music is epic and can move mountains.

My story would not have become a book without the following people: thank you to Suzanne Staszak-Silva of Rowman & Littlefield Publishers, whose enthusiasm for the project is appreciated. Thanks to my literary agents Dana Newman of Dana Newman Literary and Phyllis Parsons of The Parsons Company whose diligence and hard work made this a reality. Special thanks to Rebecca Eckland for the editing insights that expedited this project. To Lindsey Gower and Bob Yehling: Thank you for being a part of this labor of love.

To my friends and colleagues: Dan Reidenberg, Commander Aaron Werbel, Eve Myer, the Great Eric Steel, Helynna Brooke, Bob Gebbia, Muffy Walker, Author and brother-in-law Scott Hutchins, Dr. John Draper, Dr. Mel Blaustein, Paul Muller and Dr. Karin Hastik. Thank you for all the direction and guidance you have given me and for the amazing work that you do in our field.

Finally, to everyone in my life who made a tiny, small, medium or giant impact—you know who you are. Thank you from the bottom of my heart.

INTRODUCTION

~

The view from the Golden Gate Bridge is, and always has been, spectacular. When you look south toward the San Francisco skyline and west to the ocean, an opaque fog softens the view and an aggressive chill rules the air. The roadway of the Golden Gate Bridge stands at 220 feet above the waters of the bay, and the Golden Gate Bridge is one of the most internationally recognized symbols of a single city— San Francisco—and of the United States. Spanning what is called the "Golden Gate," the bridge links San Francisco to Marin County at its north. On a clear day, you can see the bridge from miles away due to its bright rusty-colored paint used to protect the iron and steel frame from erosion.

If you look down from the solid rail that lines the walkway of the bridge into the swirling currents below, the distance will seem longer than 220 feet. It will seem so far, in fact, you'll feel safe on that solid steel and iron structure which was riveted together in 1937.

Yet, I know that it takes four seconds to fall those 220 feet.

More people die by suicide from the Golden Gate Bridge than any other manmade structure in the world, and those driven to attempt suicide this way rarely survive. According to official records, as of

2005 an estimated 1,200 souls have attempted to end their lives on this vibrant red monument; that year, new suicides occurred every two weeks. In addition to surviving the trauma of such a long fall, those who jump face immediate hypothermia once they enter the frigid waters of the bay.

Official records likely differ in number from the actual suicides simply because there's no way to know how many people, driven by inner demons, have sought out the Golden Gate Bridge to perish in the oblivion offered by the dark waters below. A body can disappear without a trace from that bright, red bridge. And, in all likelihood, it's a number far greater than you or I would ever guess.

I was only nineteen years old when I attempted to end my life by jumping from the Golden Gate Bridge.

In preparation for my jump, I gave my entire comic book collection, worth nearly $5,000, to my younger brother, Joseph. I also gave away my $400 CD collection to my buddy, Jorje, a high school friend. Were I in my right mind, I would have never given away these possessions. These were items I treasured. My comic books were the friends I spent my afternoons alone with and my music gave voice to nearly every emotion I felt, whether happy or sad. Since then I've learned that giving away prized possessions exemplifies suicidal ideation, meaning the idea of suicide takes hold of people's rationalizations and they plan to kill themselves.

Yet, on the night of September 24, 2000, when I was nineteen years old and a recent high school graduate, I sat alone in my silent room, my door shut to the outside world. I made my plans while a chilling and dangerously demonic voice shouted in my head, in the space where music and comic books and happy moments spent with my family had formerly played. The voice was like the one I heard as a boy but never told anyone about its existence.

The voice that told me I had to jump from the Golden Gate Bridge.

Those who jump from the Golden Gate Bridge fall two-thirds as far as the tallest building in San Francisco's skyline, the TransAmerica building. Whatever feelings of hopelessness, of despair are soon replaced with the feeling of the rough winds that accompany such a fall. When you jump from that height, your body travels nearly seventy-five miles per hour. At that speed, wind scrapes at the skin like shards of glass.

For most, though, the harrowing realities of such a harsh death are hard to imagine when standing on the pedestrian walk that lines the roadway. Most days, it's a tourist-filled spot, where people pose for photographs with the impressive San Francisco skyline behind them. Most days, the Golden Gate Bridge walkway is lined with pedestrians or cyclists with eyes turned toward the impressive city off their right shoulder—to San Francisco. Here is where couples wrap arms around each other and photographs are taken to capture happy memories. Here is where cultures converge upon a completely American landscape, a place where memories are captured. A place that, for many, symbolizes life: or, at least, a specific time and place.

It's a place where most people look out rather than down.

Why did I jump?

The reason is quite simple. I believed, beyond a shadow of a doubt, that I had to die. I believed I had no other option. I felt as though I was a burden to my family and friends. I had no origins that I could accurately identify. I was not an athletic hero. I was not an actor. I believed I had nothing remarkable in my life.

That was, of course, not the case. I had more than plenty to live for.

Yet I had another piece of baggage—which I didn't know at the time. I had—and have—bipolar disorder.

I didn't jump because I wanted to die.

There is a huge difference between believing you have to do something and wanting to do something.

Sometimes you really want something. You want a promotion. You want a bigger house. You want to write a book. These are desires you strive for—but they are desires you create and, in some capacity, can control. It's unusual to meet a person who is compulsively writing books or compulsively working to get themselves more square footage.

Yet, sometimes you don't want something—it will not make you richer or more attractive—but you understand it is critical. These days, I run a lot. Sometimes, I get thirsty and my desire for water is critical. And, you know, it probably is—my thirst signals dehydration. My desire for water equals my physical need for it. I need water to survive and when I'm running—I need water to keep going! In that example, water is critical.

Thirteen years ago when I was nineteen and I believed I had to die, jumping from the Golden Gate Bridge was like my need for water on a long run. This belief stemmed from the arduous battle with my brain and my battle with severe mental illness. I jumped when I heard voices in my head telling me that I must die, that I had no other option.

I have bipolar type 1 disorder with psychotic features. This illness convinced me that there was no way to ease the pain except through my death.

I wonder how many other victims of the four-second fall felt as I did, that they had to die and then realized, after it was too late, that it was the worst mistake they would ever make.

They cannot write their stories.

They will never have the opportunity to tell their truths.

I write this book for those who cannot and will never give voice to their reasons or regrets.

I write this book for the families who have lost sons, daughters, mothers, and fathers to the bridge.

I write this book to anyone anywhere who has lost a loved one to the silent impulses that lie behind mental illnesses affecting families and communities all around the world.

How did I end up at this point in my life?

Based on my personal experience, suicides can be prevented. Throughout this journey, this same question is constantly on my mind as I tell my story.

I recognize that without this chapter in my life, I would be an entirely different person.

I found myself along the way.

I found my piece of hope, I came face to face with my destiny.

Most importantly, throughout this journey I found my life.

CHAPTER 1

~

The Beginning Daze

I was four months old and naked. Police officers pounding on the hotel door, where I lied, hungry and abandoned. My near-lifeless brother three feet away from me, exhausted and now quiet after screaming for hours. The police found us both on a stained, bare mattress in a hotel in San Francisco. Again, they had left us. Again, my brother started screaming. His voice gave way to a cough and it was my turn to cry; I was hungry, tired, and scared.

Only this time, the hotel manager finally called the San Francisco Police Department.

The hotel where we spent the first months of our lives was the sort of place where renters paid for rooms by the hour. These rooms were for those whose only alternative was the streets.

And that's where my parents were when the cops entered to find me and my brother, both of us scrawny and malnourished.

Small, red-faced, and screaming for our lives.

I imagine the officers turned away at first glance. They weren't heartless, but what they witnessed was the tragedy of lost innocence; children in harm's way. I was lying in my own waste for days. There may have been a sickly sweet smell in the air from our sordid conditions. Coughing from my brother, Jordache, punctuated the still air. That and the smell of Kool-Aid and Coca-Cola. Our diet.

The room was thick with the stench of neglect and sickness.

5

And this is how I entered the world.

My birth parents spent most of their waking hours in search of drugs to score, drugs to do. They had no steady income, very little food, and barely a place to stay. Their lives, by twists and turns I'll never fully know, were governed by their heavy use of drugs and alcohol.

I wish I had known them in any real sense of the word. We were both so young when members of the San Francisco Police Department placed us in foster care.

I have no tangible memories of their faces, the sounds of their voices, or of that awful place where I was found. I only have pictures and feelings of grief.

Maybe that's why I've always wondered where I come from and if it has somehow influenced my life's path.

Ever since I can remember, people asked me the question, "Why do you care what your ethnic makeup is?"

I have always replied, "You've known your entire life what your ethnic background is, right?"

"Yes," they'd respond.

"I've never known the truth. It is undeniable that knowing the truth has defined your life in some way shape or form, and knowing mine would make a big difference to me."

My birth parents were beautiful, kindhearted people who due to drugs and other behavioral health issues could leave Jordache and me unattended inside cheap rundown motels. They roamed the darkened streets and alleyways of one of America's largest cities. They occupied the shadows then, and so they do now, today, in my mind. I cannot remember either of their faces, and sometimes I find myself picking up their pictures, staring into their photographed eyes, and tearing up, hurting deeply inside. Often I cry about losing them in the way that I did, before I even gave them each the hug I always wanted to.

According to the reports I've read, the resemblance between my brother and I was uncanny. We shared the same bone structure in our faces. The same build. I wonder if these shared traits would have followed us into adulthood.

I like to imagine they would, though. And that the only difference between us was that he had curly blonde locks and I had wavy auburn hair.

I was not alone in the world. I had a brother. Once.

Years later, while attending San Jose State University in my twenties, I decided to go to a hair salon in hopes of seeing my brother as an adult. I agreed to get a full perm. My hair was normally huge and wavy at the time. I wanted curls and I wanted it naturally blonde.

The result was my normally auburn/reddish brown hair turning into the color of the California sun and curling into hundreds of loose ringlets.

I wanted to look in the mirror and see the brother barely remembered and would never know.

When I stared in the mirror, I felt his presence in the room.

But the only person in the mirror was me.

That feeling of loss swept over me again. The same feeling I had growing up. The feeling was emptiness, an absence. It would come and go throughout my life like waves.

The court decided we were better off with strangers than with our biological parents. For several months, we were. As wards of the state, we had meals to nourish us and clean sheets to sleep on. You can only imagine what this would mean to Jordache and me. We had all the things infants are supposed to have.

For a few months, we had a chance at a normal life.

We had people to tuck us in at night.

Read us bedtime stories.

Feed us infant formula and rock us to sleep when we started to cry.

It was the life we needed.

But once our biological parents were released from jail, they were desperate and did the unthinkable: they kidnapped Jordache and me. All they wanted was to stay with us, proving their love to us.

We would return to the streets, to those barren hotels.

They robbed us of food, warmth, and safety.

I remember nothing.

I only know they gave us back to the State of California. How, I still don't know.

I only know from reading what records remain that we came back smelling of sour milk. And the records show that they gave us Kool-Aid and Coca-Cola (what they could steal) once again.

My brother's cough returned.

And stayed.

Two months later, less than two years old, he died of bronchitis.

When I was twelve, I knew my birth father was already dead. However, it would be decades before I learned how my birth father died. He'd engaged in a fight with an undercover police officer while trying to score drugs, a drug deal gone badly, and he lost his life in the scuffle.

I have not gone one day of my life without thinking of my biological family. I spent nights crying myself to sleep thinking of their pain and misery during the short time they were here. I have forgiven them for their mistakes. They are the link to my past and a shining light for my present, for my future.

I had believed that my birth mother was the last link I had to my biological family. When I was twenty-seven years old I met my birth sister and brother (Shikha and Somesh). They shared with me that before she died she had found sobriety for a long period untel she turned back to drugs and died tragically.

When I lost contact with her, at age twenty-seven, I heard that she had found sobriety.

The last time she discussed anything about me to her other kids, she told them I was with a nice Russian family in Modesto. How wrong she was; it seemed she lost touch with me, too. Later—much later—I learned that my birth parents both suffered from serious mental health issues.

Debi Hines and I were destined to be mother and son.

She was the first person to visit me in the home of my former foster parents. This was long before Debi and her husband, Patrick Hines, would make the decision to adopt me.

She tells me that she saw me playing on the carpeted floor of the living room. Dressed in overalls, my hands lifted and tossed an old blue horseshoe throwing plastic toy into the air, trying to land it on its white stub over where the yellow and red, orange and green horseshoes.

I couldn't crawl due to my severe malnourishment. My stomach was distended.

But Debi Hines was touched and saw her little boy.

She says that was the moment she "fell in love."

And although the first child she took in, Elizabeth, was only eight months older than me, and friends warned Debi that the close age difference "wasn't natural," she came to see me again but only once.

Although I couldn't crawl.

But there was something about me. Or something about *us*. Instead of listening to her friends and family, Debi Hines remained longer than expected, watching the tiny toddler toss plastic colored horseshoes into the air. I might have laughed—I was happy, warm, and clothed for the first time in my life. That was all the convincing she needed.

Debi Hines decided I was going to be her son, despite protests from friends.

The last time my birth mother saw me, she was drunk. Wanting to keep my biological mother a part of my life, Debi Hines scheduled visits through a court-appointed social worker. When Debi arrived, she found my mother slumped in a chair against the wall in the lobby of the Department of Social Services building. Her eyes were blood-shot and red. She smelled of alcohol.

She stood on shaky legs and took me from Debi's arms and said to the man who had been sitting beside her: "This is my baby."

Then she called me Jordache, the name of my dead brother.

Her eyes went vacant as though she was no longer present in her body. The silence was eerie and Debi was afraid she'd forget she was holding me.

"Are you OK?" Debi asked her.

My birthmother began to cry. Then, her face contorted into an ugly sneer and she said: "Get away from me. Get out of my sight, I can't stand you." She paused as tears rolled down her cheeks, holding me out with straight arms so she could look at all of me at once. Then she said: "I'm going to kill myself, but you live, you live."

Each time I saw my biological mom, I cried. I had grown attached to Debi and her gentle, caring demeanor. She gave me everything I could ever want—food, warm clothing, and not just shelter, but a *home*.

For nearly two years, Debi took me to see my biological mother at the Department of Social Services. There was a chance, it seems, that I could be returned to my biological parents.

During this time, the only things my biological mother gave me were: a wooden block that had belonged to Jordache, a broken plastic car, a banana, pork rinds, and half a box of chocolate-covered cherries.

But as they say, when God closes a door, He opens a window.

How true that was for me.

Patrick and Debi Hines filed suit and won their case against my birth parents. They saved me from dingy motels and a life no kid wants to imagine as their own. Almost like a fairytale, they swept me up and gave me a life most can only dream about.

We lived in a beautiful home that was, as a rule, immaculately clean. I had siblings to keep me company, and parents who were home when I was.

Most importantly, however, Patrick and Debi were the first individuals who fought for my future and battled to save my life.

Patrick Kevin Hines is a stern half-Irish, half-German man. He is very tall, standing at six feet one inch. However, it is not his height that makes him larger than life—it's his personality.

He speaks like an astute history buff. He wears fashionable and expensive tortoise shell prescription glasses. The man garners his specific style from San Francisco's oldest and most upscale clothing places.

His clothes and glasses remind me of Robert De Niro's character in the movie *The Good Shepherd*, about the birth of the CIA. His character was classic and filled with strength, anger, and the right amount of gruff, just like my dad. In fact, if it weren't for his blond hair now turning white, my father would resemble the mannerisms and expressions of the great De Niro and his many characters. Next to De Niro, my father is spot-on for the acclaimed Seymour Hoffman profile. If only I had the ability to stand next to all three masculine, passionate men, a dream film of mine would come true.

My dad is the kind of man who had to earn everything he ever wanted the hard way. He played goalie for a semi-pro hockey team for years—without a mask. I like to joke that some may find that a bit tough, but I just called it silly. Some of his teeth were replaced because of it.

He grew up in a privileged home. His father, a naval officer, went away to fight in the Battle of Okinawa. When his father returned home some years later, he was a changed man. He could not adapt to civilian life. He had seen way too much for far too long. He started the family's longshoreman's business upon his return. After a few years the business failed. He and his wife, my grandmother, turned straight to the bottle.

They would soon be consumed by alcohol.

Dad had to attend grammar school and keep his younger sister safe at the same time. He paid his way through some of his high school years and funded his own collegiate career. He worked his way up from making chocolate bananas in a 1960s candy store to making ice for the ice follies and hockey games, eventually finding more gainful employment. He supported his little sister until she was whisked away by his grandmother because she was the "favorite" grandchild... and my dad was not. She literally did not like him. In fact, she would send him a penny on his birthday as a gift just to spite him. And my dad, well, he would send it right back to her.

When my dad turned seventeen, he moved into the crappy basement of someone's home and paid his own bills. Somehow he worked his way into the University of San Francisco after nearly being kicked out of City College for "maintaining" a .01 GPA during the Vietnam War draft years. His GPA was low because he had to work so hard to be able to make his rent payments and to live on his own. You have to remember—he was only a seventeen-year-old "kid."

After suffering through his parents' alcoholism and not experiencing a normal family life, my dad wanted what he had lost. Nothing was acceptable but working diligently, swiftly, and intelligently for his future, and for his future family.

One of the most memorable lessons I learned from my dad comes from his work and life experiences. He taught me that it is not nearly enough to want, hope, or wish to succeed. These abstract thoughts do not come close to achieving true success. It is careless to feel entitled to receiving a fortune just because those circumstances were once a part of your life; just like it's useless to feel hopeless without them. If your mother and father have money now or have had money all of their lives, your life is not necessarily set for you, no matter how much money you came from or are positioned to inherit.

He always reminded me that anything can happen and everything can change.

Patrick and Debi Hines also adopted two other children, Elizabeth and Joseph. Elizabeth and I were adopted together, although she was taken in before me, and Joseph was adopted later.

My brother, Joseph, is from a black family. My sister, Elizabeth, is of European-American descent. According to my mom, I loved Elizabeth the first time I saw her.

Together, we lived a life of privilege, particularly during the holidays. Christmas Day was packed with an abundance of toys and new clothes in boxes with wrapping and ribbons beneath the tree that twinkled with multicolored lights and smelled like evergreen. My first Christmas with the Hines family found me wearing navy blue shorts, saddle shoes, and a bow tie.

What waited for me beneath the tree was usually an assortment of my favorite things: He-Man, Spider-Man, GI Joe, and Transformer action figures.

Elizabeth squealed with joy, seated next to me, as she tore open packages revealing My Little Pony—miniature pastel-colored horses—and Care Bares with their colorful stomachs and rainbow-colored fur.

There were always three stockings hanging from the mantle. They had been empty the night before, but come Christmas morning, we'd find them stuffed to the brim with candy canes, colorful Pez dispensers of our favorite characters, comic books, and other miscellaneous items.

Everything we wanted and more was there. Spread out beneath the twinkling lights of the Christmas tree, dripping with ornaments and silver-colored tinsel, which fell so deep into the carpet my mom was still vacuuming it out of the carpet in March.

In so many ways, it was more than any of us could have ever imagined.

Every Easter, too, was a family affair with handfuls of cousins who joined Libby, Joseph, and me in the search of the Easter basket that contained the most candy and chocolate at Grandma Kay and Papa Jack's house. We searched in every direction—around the trimmed hedges and early grass grown long under the constant spring rains for the basket we knew existed, somewhere.

We knew it would be *big* because it always was, every year.

We knew it would be filled with chocolate-covered eggs and gifts wrapped in pastel-colored paper for each of us. Chocolate-covered rabbits and small gifts you treasure as a kid that you can hardly remember as a grownup.

When we found it—big and brimming with treats—we wasted no time stuffing our faces, covering our fingers in dark brown, sticky, melted chocolate. We didn't know how good we had it.

And then there were Thanksgivings.

That third week in November.

The shuffle of adults into the kitchen where talk and the clinking of glasses kept any other noise inaudible.

The smell of turkey—warm and lightly spiced like home—filled every room and even found its way outside where my Libby, my cousins, and I launched ourselves into piles of crunchy leaves that had fallen from the trees in the yard.

The table, made longer by extra pieces placed in to it, held chairs on every side. The plates were filled with turkey. Stuffing. Cranberry sauce from a can that was cut into round slices.

Thanksgiving became a great big party with all of the extended family in one place eating, talking, and arguing about politics, religion, and lifestyles.

But Halloween was always my favorite. That was the holiday I was allowed to dress like the person I always wanted to be: the hero.

Sometimes I was the powerful He-Man, the amazing Spider-Man. On other Halloweens I dressed like GI Joe generals. Or even a robotic Transformer.

All those big and powerful superheroes, in one way or another, had saved the human race more than once.

I remember on Halloween we would wake up early, put on our costumes, my dad would paint our faces and then he would take us to school.

Near the end of the day, each class would have a Halloween party, the kind where parents brought cupcakes with orange frosting or gave us hand-shaped bags filled with popcorn and candy corn at the tips of each finger, posing as faux fingernails.

Then, my mother would pick us up and take us home.

We wore our costumes while we did our homework.

We also wore them while we ate our dinner. It's not often you have a princess and Spider-Man over for dinner, but one night each year, our family did.

And the trick or treating. We lived in a neighborhood you could still trick or treat in today. Where neighbors knew each other and the well-lit sidewalks and streets were filled with families doing exactly the same thing.

Mom and Dad took us trick or treating on Halloween night, leading us from one front door to the next. They would alternate letting Libby and I ring the doorbell. We would visit all of our family and friends' homes where we would get an extra handful of treats after we shouted in unison: "Trick or treat!"

Everyone was so generous with their hospitality, candy, and kindness. Mom and Dad were careful about checking our candy before letting us eat any.

Over the years, my MO didn't change much. I must have been Spider-Man, a swashbuckling pirate, or Dracula two or three times each, although I do remember that I dressed up like the grim reaper two years in a row.

My dad was always immersed in my costume creating process, though, especially for me. Usually my mom took care of Joseph and Libby's costumes, but I remember my dad painting the greatest Spider-Man face on the planet. It almost won me the school costume contest. One of the years I took second place.

I remember so much about this, in part, because my dad would use his videocassette recorder to capture all of these terrific moments and costumes. It's funny to watch them now: each year Spider-Man got a little taller, growing into his superhero body.

No matter the costume, however, in these videos I'm always smiling.

I still have the videos my dad taped. Heck, I even still have the camera.

I remember how much Dad liked to make those holiday home videos. If it were a special moment, Dad would bring out the camera.

Every holiday, birthday, or special event. We have them all recorded because of him.

After all, he was the director and writer of those days. All of the family was privy to his filmmaking skills. As we grew older, he played these home movies to remind us of the fun, exciting, or very embarrassing moments in our lives.

If dad was the director, then mom was the artistic producer.

I will never forget the children's book *The Little Engine That Could*. Growing up, we knew we could succeed because of my mom and dad always reading about and proclaiming it. One of the other books she read repeatedly to us was *Love You Forever*. The main line in the book goes something like, "I will like you forever, I will love you for always, until the end of time my baby you'll be."

Those were the closing lines before she would turn the light off in my room at night. It was the line that would set me on the path to good dreams, snuggled beneath warm He-Man or Spider-Man blankets and sheets.

She also sang these words whenever I felt down: "Pick yourself up, dust yourself off, and start all over again."

And how can I forget when she belted out Doris Day's "Que Sera Sera"? I cannot speak for my brother and sister, but as much as I pretended to hate it—groaning or rolling my eyes when I heard those familiar words set to a familiar tune—I didn't.

I still sing this, again and again, in my head when life goes south. She does not know how much her songs meant to me as I got older, or how often I turn to the words in those books for guidance. I even recite the words "I think I can, I think I can" as an adult in tough situations.

What I remember most about growing up, though, is Elizabeth. She had beautiful rosy cheeks and curly blond pigtails. Happiness exuded from within her as a small child, as it did from me. Of all the members of the Hines clan, I bonded with Elizabeth first.

Much later, when we officially became a member of the Hines clan and could speak, I called my older sister Ibby-Bee because I could not say the name "Elizabeth." It soon morphed into Libby. Our entire family—immediate and extended—followed suit. I totally made up my sister's name!

Libby was so smart. She had, and still has, such quick wit.

She wrote the most sensational poetry and was a creative-minded child. We were best friends as little kids, absolutely inseparable. I followed her everywhere she went.

When she said "Jump," I asked "How high?"

Once, when we were visiting our mountain cabin near the lake, she suggested she tie me to a tree while she got the hose and would spray me with it.

"OK!" I beamed, while she wrapped the rope around my torso, holding me fast to the trunk of a pine tree.

She walked to the spigot calmly, knowing that I wouldn't try to break free and run. I'd agreed to do what she asked and I was a kid of my word.

I watched her turn and face me, hose in one hand.

"Are you ready?" she asked.

I nodded, encouraging her to spray me.

And she did, with what seemed to be filled with below freezing cold water.

I might have complained, but Libby squealed with delight. Then I started laughing, too.

Our other adventures included her accepting me into her room as she described her imaginary closet friend, and how she would, on a daily basis disappear for hours into an imaginary world within her closet. Only to Libby, it wasn't just a closet: it was a world filled with unicorns and fairies.

It was a magical land.

As we grew older, things changed.

When we were in grammar school, the girls in Libby's class teased her relentlessly. Or, if they weren't teasing and hazing her, they were ignoring her entirely. Some of the boys at her school called her "little chubby cheeks."

Initially, she brushed it all off, but "little chubby cheeks" followed her through every grade.

Libby lost her self-esteem.

Every day, she would come home with her cheeks already tear-streaked, retreat to her bedroom, and sob.

Our mom and dad always tried to console her. Mom tried to sing "Pick yourself up" to her, but it didn't seem to help Libby.

Libby had always been sensitive and forgiving, but she never learned how to leave behind struggles with her inner demons. She developed a distorted self-image believing, even in grade school, that she was too chubby and fat.

When Libby was nine years old, she started using food as punishment for all the things she thought were wrong with her. For every test she failed to ace, for every time a boy or girl would call her "chubby cheeks," the lunch our mom had packed for her would be left un-touched, tossed into the nearest trash.

No one asked her about it; coming home empty-handed had always meant, before, that the lunch our mom had packed had been eaten.

After each day she "failed" to do something, she would come home and "slow down" her eating. At dinner while our plates' contents diminished at about the same rate, Libby's plate was always mysteriously filled.

"Your dinner's getting cold," my dad might say, thinking Libby was imagining something again and had simply forgotten to eat.

Later, the critiques of my parents became more pointed. "Quit dawdling!" my mom would say.

In response, Libby would pick up her fork again, and move the food around her plate, spearing the smallest morsel as though she would take a bite. And when she was sure the family's attention had moved on to something else, she'd lower the fork again, leaving the food untouched.

In fact, it seemed as if it took hours for her eat a meal that most of us finished in minutes. Eventually, we'd give up and when we were not watching she would scrape her uneaten plate into the trash.

The truth was that she was not finishing her meals at all. So many things seemed beyond her control—the teasing and name-calling at school, inability to score perfectly on exams. The only thing she thought she could control was if she ate or didn't eat.

By the time she was twenty-nine, Libby had been battling bulimia and anorexia nervosa for twenty years. Her clothes that had once fit her now hung like empty sacks from her skeletal frame. Her face—those round cheeks—were no longer there. In their place were hollowed cheekbones that cast sharp shadows over her face. Her eyes were worn and drawn, tired and old looking. Her smile disappeared. No longer filled with happiness, her face was an expression of pain.

She was admitted to a treatment facility where physicians, psychiatrists, and therapists helped her slowly find her way to health.

Soon thereafter, everything changed. Despite having gained weight—though not nearly enough to appear recognizable—she came down with what was thought to be an untreatable food-borne illness. Within weeks, she lost all of the weight she had gained. Once again, she became dangerously thin.

She suffered mentally with the contradictory thoughts of those with disordered eating. She wanted to be healthy and well, but those inner demons still told her she would become "fat" if she ate too much.

One option remained. The medical professionals who attended her had tried to have Libby eat, but she couldn't keep food down. A feeding tube was placed in her stomach. When I visited her, I remember that I could distinctly see every one of Libby's ribs.

At barely four feet eleven her condition was life threatening. At one point, she stopped breathing on her own. She was eventually admitted to the psychiatric unit of a hospital in Petaluma.

She worked hard to recover while under the doctors' care and was able to regain enough weight to return home that Christmas. She learned how to enjoy food again without it hurting her, increasing her body mass for the first time in more than two decades.

We were all so proud of her. The family realized that every day was a battle for Elizabeth. A battle that, if lost, could take her life.

Just like my own battle with demons.

I was a bright, happy-go-lucky, run-amok kid who loved to play and loved my caring and tight-knit family life. Our closeness was obvious to anyone. Sure, like everyone on this earth, my mom and dad have their flaws: my father's temper that can flare or my mom's impatience and perfectionism. But our happiness trumped them all.

Every summer, we traveled to "our" lake, three and a half hours north of San Francisco. The lake was a place of fun and solace, "our little slice of heaven" as my mom used to say.

Our spot was in a small trailer park area and we leased the land. We were right on the lake, and tied to our dock was our motorboat and two sailboats. When it rained too much in that area during the winter, our cabin was nearly flooded, the downside of living so close to the lake. The water seemed to barely miss us every year.

However, during the summer our place was the envy of the rest. Our cabin was beige with brown trim. It had a sliding glass door in the front and a metal door with a screen in the back.

I was always in charge of cleaning the patio upon arrival, using the electric blower as a broom and rake to remove the fall leaves and a duster to move out all of the spiders and bugs that had made our spot theirs. My mom taught a lot about responsibility at the lake. She told me I had to clean before I played, and when I got older, I had to complete homework before hanging out with my summer friends.

After finishing the chores, I would transform into "Chief Run-Amok," my alter ego. I would collect duck feathers, and my mom or dad would tie them on to a bandanna and wrap that bandanna around my head. As "Chief Run-Amok," I ran around, imagining myself the chief of my own Indian tribe.

My grandparents had a place two doors down from us. Friends and extended family would join us at various times throughout the warm summer months. Those are some of my greatest and fondest memories.

I met Jesse Greer at the lake, a person who would become one of my very best friends. His family owned the part where our cabin was located. We were not friends at first. When we were both a bit older I would see him working with his father on the grounds. In fact, that's how we became pals. I was using the leaf blower to clean the porch when I noticed another kid my age mowing the lawns on the grounds, a huge job. I stopped the leaf blower, letting the mountain sounds fill the air again.

"Hey!" I said, waving my hand at Jesse.

He looked up from his task of making the lawns look neat and crisp then waved back. He didn't turn off his mower, though. And once he'd waved back, his attention returned to the task at hand. I never knew someone that young with such a great work ethic.

On Jessie's off time, he and I used to lift weights in the giant silver metal shed at the top of the hill next to the black iron entrance gate. The weights had belonged to his dad. The red-covered bench press had a hole in it, but that didn't matter—it was still my favorite lift to do with Jesse.

When we weren't working out, we would speedboat race in his baby blue boat, swim on one of the three main docks, or dive together for clams. Or, we'd head off to the only resort on the lake and a favorite hangout.

Although we weren't technically allowed to swim in one of resort's four pools unless we were actual guests of the resort, Jesse and I along with practically every other family from the park always got into the pool via a white handlebar-mustached lifeguard named "Bob." After walking the short mile from our cabin, Bob would open the gate and gesture for us to come inside. At first we went to the pool for their Saturday karaoke scene were I'd do my best impression of Elvis's "You Ain't Nothing but a Hound Dog."

Later, though, when I'd gotten too old and too "cool" for karaoke, the pool became the place where Jesse and I would try and master the mysterious art of "the pickup" on the bikini-clad girls that populated the resort's poolside each summer season.

There was a serious competition between Jesse and me for who could get the new girls our age to hook up with one of us at or near the park.

I was never as successful as Jesse was with the ladies. Whereas he would close the deal, I would become the "nice guy friend" or the guy who never got past getting a girl's phone number, or at most, a kiss on the cheek.

Even so, I did eventually meet my first two girlfriends at the lake.

Both pretended to dislike me at first. When I'd ask if they wanted to go waterskiing or wake boarding, they would give me a look that said: "As if!"

Yet, with both girls it was mere weeks before they revealed their true feelings.

I remember the first, a sunny blonde, who reversed the order of "the pickup." One day, she asked while sitting on one of the docks: "Do you want go out with me?"

I misunderstood the gist of her question, believing that she just wanted to go somewhere. *That's a weird thing to ask*, I thought to myself. *There are not a lot of places here to go to. The town only has one stoplight!*

And so, I replied, perplexed: "Where will we go?" I wondered if she wanted to sing karaoke, or to eat at the only "nice" restaurant around— the one that sold greasy-fried stuff or to grab a Slurpee-type drink from the snack bar.

I had no idea she wanted to be my girlfriend.

The lake was my haven, it invigorated me, it made me so happy. My mind was clear. I felt pure joy. A time when I lived completely well.

Each fall when we returned from a summer at the lake, Elizabeth and I went to our church's private school. The school population was predominantly Caucasian. The students were mostly white Irish and Italian families and only a few Asian Americans. During my time there, only one black student attended the school. Unbeknownst to everyone, including myself, the school was more ethnically diverse because of my background, my heritage.

As I've said before, my past was a mystery to me until I was twenty-seven years old.

At our school, the students in various grades bullied and teased me because I did not look like them. Instead of having blonde or brown hair, I stuck out like a sore thumb with my wavy auburn color, my ears and nose that both seemed too large for my head, my tan, freckled skin. One of those traits—or all of them—seemed to incite their wrath. Or, maybe it was simply the fact that I was neither 100 percent Irish or Italian. I wasn't 100 percent of anything.

Every day, I was harassed and called a "red nigger" by older students. By their racial slurs, I gleaned they assumed that I was part black. Later, I learned that many were the children of a bigoted group. Even as a sixth-grade kid, these eighth graders saw me as an outsider.

I felt this way, too, in part, because of my dad. Every day he drove me to school, pulling close to the curb at the school's front ramp leading into the schoolyard. In plain view of everyone, he'd reach into his back left pocket for his overstuffed money clip. Unfurling the bills, he'd slip one across the seat to me. Always a twenty-dollar bill for the day.

I hated it, taking the money and hiding it in one of my pockets, hoping no one had seen what had just occurred.

It made me feel privileged—different than the other students—and I thought I didn't deserve to be. I would think of those who couldn't feed themselves, or house and clothe their families.

I would also think of my biological mom and dad, who had little to nothing. I don't know why or how, but his actions as a prominent financial expert made me think that this caretaking gesture was not acceptable. I started to refuse to take the twenty-dollar bill from him even though, every day, he would reach for the folded bills, unfurl them and hand a twenty to me.

After about a month of refusing to take the money offered to me, my dad said: "Money doesn't grow on trees, and I earn every penny. It isn't given to you to boast. We're blessed that I make the money I do. You should be thankful for what we have. You're in *middle school*; you don't earn anything. I might not always make this kind of money, but I do now. It's not charity, it's for family, it's for you, take it."

I nodded and reached out, taking the twenty-dollar bill and folding it carefully before putting it in my pocket. I finally understood.

I was too young to be prideful about money. He wanted to give me what he didn't have growing up. Or, what I might not have had, if he and my mom hadn't wanted to adopt me so badly. Anyway, he was right: I had no way to earn it myself.

At our school some of the other students would hold me down and beat me up. Everywhere they could. There was nowhere I could escape their calling me every name in the book.

Before and after school when there were no teachers or parents in sight, they would push me to the ground and my palms would collect the grains of loose gravel in them as I'd try to pick myself up again. Once down, they'd chant taunts and racial slurs. "Ginger." "Red nigger."

That went on for all seven years I attended this school, without check.

Eventually, of course, I got fed up with the name-calling and being pushed around. Unfortunately, there wasn't anything that I alone could do about it. A group of the other students had joined forces against me.

One day, I walked through the recess area on my way to class when suddenly another student grabbed me from behind and held my arms. I struggled, trying to worm my way free. I hardly noticed the other student approaching from the left until it was too late. It was my main bully, an Italian built like a square, brick building.

I struggled harder to get away, already knowing what was coming. But the student behind me was strong and I couldn't seem to gain any space between his body and mine or to get my arms back to where I needed them.

My bully said nothing as he approached. It was almost mechanical the way he pulled his arm back and let it lose toward me, full force. He began punching me in the stomach, hard punches that sent waves of pain throughout my body. One blow, a second, and then he'd say "Ginger" (a red-haired kid with freckles). He'd say it again and again until tears streamed down my face.

That's what they had all been waiting for.

Maybe I was the sort of kid who is always, inevitably, bullied.

After all, I was also an awkward and overly sensitive kid. It's not that I wasn't an athlete—I was. I played on several of the school's "B" teams. Granted, I wasn't among the best (that would be the "A" team) but I can't claim I wasn't fit and strong, too, for my age. It's just that I spent a lot of time drawing—something other boys my age didn't do. And then there were my huge ears and a gigantic nose, too large for my face, that followed me year after year in school. Such easy targets for schoolyard drama.

Despite all the bullying, the years at the private school provided me with great learning experience. It was at this school, in fact, where I remember seeing my first public speech. I was in the seventh grade and my father gave a keynote address on Career Day. As I watched my dad on the stage, I remember thinking to myself: I wish I could do that some day. Little did I know that through the major events that were to occur in my life in the years that followed that I would become a public speaker.

Also at our private school I learned how not to treat people by learning what it was like to be an outcast.

The friends I made at this school became "true" friends: there was Oscar Navarro, an Italian and Irish lanky kid, who lived down the block from school. He had bright red hair and a spunky attitude to match. I also met Len Mason, an uncoordinated fellow who was teased for his height despite being the kindest and gentlest giant I've ever known. I also met "Too Tall" Jon who did not attend the same high school as I did, but who nonetheless became a lifelong friend.

Yet, Oscar and Len landed in the same boat I was consistently thrown into. They were just as miserable at our school and just as fearful of bullies.

Since it became quite obvious I was never going to be popular, I turned my focus onto other things, like becoming an artist. Drawings and doodles soon covered the front and inside of my school notebooks.

Superheroes were my favorite characters to sketch because I fantasized about becoming one someday—to the point where I was often lost in my own daydreams at school. Often, teachers would ask me a question, and I'd look up, blinking.

I had no idea what the answer was.

I had been in my own world.

So, many of my teachers thought I was a bad listener. I was held back a year, thinking I had more to learn from taking kindergarten a second time around.

That wasn't the case, though. Really, I was just more focused on my inner world where I was a hero than the outside one where I was bullied because of how I looked and acted.

There was also another reason for my "bad" listening skills: a reason that wouldn't come to the attention of teachers or even my family until I was seventeen years old. My brain was moving faster than a "healthy" human brain should. I was (unknowingly at the time) dealing with serious rapid and tangential thought patterns. I heard every word said by my teachers, family, classmates, and friends.

Every word.

Unlike a "normal" child, though, I overanalyzed every piece of information as it worked its way through my brain.

Every word.

Not only every word, I heard every consonant and vowel. Every part of speech—verbs, nouns, and adjectives—uttered in conversations, separated by the intonation, volume, and inflection of each voice.

Every voice.

I grew confused and bewildered by the sounds and gestures around me. To others, I appeared to be zoning out or "not paying any attention" when, really, I was paying attention to every detail in the world around me.

It was painful.

Sometimes, I could not answer teachers because I was so tormented by trying to parse the meaning of all those outside voices. Some call it attention deficit disorder (ADD).

I call it madness.

When I was fifteen, I applied and was accepted into a prestigious all-boys Catholic school. My father graduated from the school in 1967. It was quite inspiring for me to see his graduation picture in the hallway while I was at the school. He was the only one in his class with 1960s' Ray-Bans on. Going to this high school was a wonderful experience for me—for the first two years, anyway.

My freshman year, I weighed a sliver over 100 pounds. I was five feet two inches tall. I remember that I was lean and had a six-pack. It was a physical goal of mine for which I had strived since sixth grade, imitating my heroes.

Even though I loved the school, I once again became the target of bullies. They made fun of my head, which was physically huge. My ears and nose seemed to grow exponentially without my head catching up or my body following suit. Taking all of this into account and keeping mostly positive, I was still very excited to be in a new arena with all the new faces and the potential to make new friends.

My entrance into this high school gave my mother a big smile.

She felt confident that I would get into the school and spread my wings in the all-boys Catholic environment. She thought I would excel in acting and academics. I would excel at everything I put my mind to there, she said.

At the time, I felt it was a huge sacrifice giving up girls for high school. In fact, I hesitated before turning in my application, wondering if I really wanted to surround myself with only other guys my age.

But I did apply, thinking that this was where I ought to be. Their academic and extracurricular activities were stellar and well known.

Yet, I remember how hard it was to fit in at first. When I entered the main cafeteria for lunch, I would look around, trying to find out where, or rather who, I would sit with.

It became clear that I had to choose carefully.

The tables were commandeered by ethnic groups. The black table stood to the right. I walked over, feeling that I could relate. They looked at me as if to say, "You buddy, are not black enough to sit here." Then, I turned to the far right of the room to the Filipino, or Asian, table. The occupants of this table looked to me with deadeye stares. One student who had seen my searching eyes said "Hey pal, you've really got the wrong table!"

Then I found the "white" table. I began to sit down when a young, very tall, Irish student named Ryan stopped me. "Hey, what are you?"

"What do you mean?" I asked.

"What is your background?"

At the time I had been misinformed by my adoption documents and thought that I was East Indian, English, and Italian. That is exactly what I told him.

He immediately blurted out, "You're East Indian, and you can't sit here!"

One student, Arthur said, "Dude, don't listen to him, you are welcome to sit here." Another added, "Don't worry about him he doesn't know what he's talking about. Take a seat."

I've never liked being associated with cliques. But I found myself right smack in the middle of one. Unlike the other boys who had all grown up together, attending a neighboring grammar school, I was the outsider. Yet, faced with the alternative of having nowhere to sit, I slid onto a seat between Arthur and Denis, which is where I'd sit every day for all the days I attended ARHS—Archbishop Riordan High School.

Although those boys became my friends and I eventually "fit in" just as much as they did, it was during that time that I had my first breakdown.

It was the first time others and myself became aware of my battle with mental instability.

Unlike my mom, my father was not as ecstatic about my decision to only apply to the all-boys Catholic school. He, much like any proud father, wanted me to have a few other options in case this option fell through. Originally, he wanted me to consider another school, one that I felt it would be an extension of our private school, with the students being mostly white and intolerant of anyone they perceived to be different.

Believe me, I *was* different and stood out like a sore thumb.

As a youngster and teenager, I was simply looked upon as a "friggin' meat ball"—as my friend Ryan used to call me, meaning I was the goof ball, the class clown. By this time in my life, I could have cared less about sports or football. In my freshman year, I joined the diversity group and the theater department. I even joined the debate team for a couple of weeks. I was horrible.

Instead of researching my debate topics, I would show up unprepared. Debaters were supposed to act like trial lawyers, defending their point with clear, logical arguments. But, because I never prepared for these debates, I could never make my point and half the time I couldn't see the point myself.

Public speaking, I believed, just wasn't my "thing."

My sophomore year, while serving on the Diversity Committee, I traveled with five or six other students to the country's Annual Diversity Committee Conference in Denver, Colorado. There, I saw a presenter who would change the course of my life.

He was the keynote speaker of the day. A young black man, he strode onto the stage with a cool swagger with dark sunglasses on, wearing a loose navy blue colored velour jumpsuit. In his mound of an afro rested a pick comb, slightly askew. He carried a boom box, blasting hip hop music throughout the room.

He cast a glance over all of us before saying, in an accentuated-tone filled with slang: "So, whatch-y'all think of me?"

Some of the audience members nodded. Most of us smirked, wondering where this presentation was going.

But as abruptly and noisily as his presentation had begun, the speaker stopped.

He stopped speaking with slang.

He turned off the boom box and set it at his feet.

He unzipped and stepped out of the velour jumpsuit, revealing a crisp suit and tie, freshly pressed and tailored.

He took off the afro—which had been just a wig—to reveal trimmed hair and placed a pair of eyeglasses on his face. Casting another glance across the room, he asked in a clear and carefully articulated voice: "What do all of you think of me now?"

Nearly all of us gasped at the transformation that had occurred.

"Perception can change your life. You are perceived by how you look and sound," he said. He told us about his experience with the power of perception—how his whole life he was perceived as uneducated and unsophisticated simply because of the color of his skin. Despite his high school and college degrees, he said he was always assumed to be less of a person than he was.

And his life's work, ever since, was about changing that not just for himself, but for every audience he reached.

Something inside me clicked after hearing his presentation. Not only was I inspired by the message he offered, I was inspired by the way he delivered it: as a public speaker. A spark was lit that I would return to years later.

High school.

I remember wanting to be on the wrestling team and in theater productions. From the get-go, my father begged me to play football. He dreamed of it.

Football was his passion. His dream, a dream that sadly ended at the age of eleven. My father did not have the same luxuries that I was blessed with. Instead, my dad had to work, focusing on supporting himself and, later, his family.

Instead of living out his dream, and much to his chagrin, I joined the diversity group and the theater department. Then wrestling fell into my lap. Wrestling was the sport for which my high school was known and excelled at.

In my freshman year, I lost nearly every match but, like my father had always taught me, I always got up off the mat. I always went to practice and competed in every match.

Slowly, I improved.

During my sophomore year, wrestling at the junior varsity level, I won first place in our hometown tournament.

My dad was very proud of these athletic accomplishments.

My mother, on the other hand, did not comprehend the sport. It seemed odd to her. She didn't understand the points versus pin system. She would have preferred that I stayed focused on drama. There are days that she still wishes that I would.

I'll never forget the day of my championship. It's as though I am still standing on the purple and gold floor. I can still smell the air and how it seemed laced with excitement and anticipation. The sounds of the referees who called the matches and the slap of skin as it fell to the mat, held pinned in defeat. The clanging of the bell to signal the round had ended.

I paced back and forth in the locker room before taking the mat, listening to DMX's 1998 number one album "It's Dark and Hell is Hot" on my CD player. That was what I always listened to, then, to get pumped up.

When it was time, I de-robed and weighed in.

I made weight by less than two pounds; if I were hair over, I would have moved up to the next weight class to face bigger, stronger opponents. I would have been in trouble.

I looked around at the other teams and the people I had wrestled that year. I saw a guy from who beat me last season in duals.

Or, "pummeled me" might be a better way to describe it.

The dude was scary. He had a red and yellow Superman "S" tattooed on his right shoulder, but I was not fazed. My season record of twenty-two wins and six losses spoke for itself. Finally, I was a contender.

The best wrestler in my weight category went up to the scale smiling at me with an evil grin. We were wrestling at 130 pounds. I had lifted weights all year to achieve that number. He looked at me as if he were going to pound my body into the floor. I was nervous but excited, knowing how much I'd improved over the course of the season. I walked up to the tournament board and saw my opponents, the same guys who had beaten me before.

"Shit!" I blurted out loud.

My favorite head coach, Theodore White said, "Cool it, you are gonna do fine, trust me."

Theodore is a man of great passion and has an insatiable drive to win. More important than his drive to win, he wants everyone on his team to have fun and learn a lot during their tenure on the team. He is an intelligent guy with a knack for bringing out the best in his students and team members. The day of my tournament I also had my family in the bleachers to cheer me on.

My first match was against some guy I didn't know from a team I didn't recognize. I took him out in what seemed like seconds. "One, two, three, pin!"

The bell clanged, calling the match.

My teammates cheered me on but instead of yelling my name, they all yelled: "Rocky, Rocky, Rocky!" like Dwayne "The Rock" Johnson himself. From the time I had entered high school up until this point, I was a huge Rock fan, I walked the school hallways spouting of all of Dwayne's catch phrases successfully dubbing myself the school's "Rocky."

The first match left me electrified. With new energy and confidence, I thought I just might be able to do it. I might be able to win.

I could hardly stand to wait for my next match, which was twenty minutes away.

I had to stay pumped: my next opponent was from the same school as the guy who pummeled me earlier in the year. I saw a little shrimp of a kid trying to stay as pumped as I was.

I knew he was done. I took my place on the mat and immediately swung the shrimp around, pinning him beneath my weight and strength. The chanting from the stands grew louder and more aggressive. "One, two, three, pin!" I did it again.

"Rocky, Rocky, Rocky!" they cheered as the ref held up my arm. Once again, I'd won my match.

I drew the next card which would determine my final match of the day. I read the name and my heart sank. It was a sneering muscle-bound dude. I wondered how this guy could have made weight. He looked as big as a house. He looked like he was on steroids. I had another twenty-minute wait until my next round. I listened to my CD again. I tried not to let my nerves jump out of my skin.

As the minutes trickled by, I couldn't believe I was going for the gold. I didn't have a chance.

I stepped onto the mat and into the circle. My opponent looked like an animal, a beast, like the X-Men's Logan, or "Wolverine," out for blood, but with blonde locks and without the sideburns. I must have been visibly afraid because inside, I was trembling. I tried to disguise my fear with a false bravado. I hoped it worked.

The referee asked us to shake hands.

My opponent gritted his perfect white choppers. He was from a team of behemoths and wrestling monsters. The yellow and brown of his uniform crisscrossed down his singlet with his school's letters in white on the upper right chest. He was ready to take me out like he had the last time. He looked at me as though he expected an easy victory. However, I wasn't having any of that nonsense.

The whistle blew. We were interlocked. My mind was racing. He was so much stronger. I prayed, *God please don't let me lose the championship in front of my entire family, all of my classmates, friends, coaches, and teammates.* He took me down, nearly pinning me almost immediately. This happened in the first fifteen seconds of the match. Everyone thought it was over.

Everyone was wrong. I had what I can only describe as a rush of pure adrenaline-filled rage. I reversed his motion and I took top position. He would not repeat his win from the previous season. He could no longer beat me! I was too determined.

The coaches yelled as they always did in practice, "Do you want it more, or does he? Show us you want it more!"

I then pulled off what I called "The Kevin Hines Special." It was a wrestling move that would later be called the "Almer," after a senior who used the move with such perfection he won nearly every one of his matches with it.

I locked my right arm above his neck and around his head and sprawled my legs out behind me. I then took my left arm and put it through his right arm and rolled him on his back.

I pushed, but no matter how hard I pushed, he would not go all the way down. One of his shoulders never touched the mat.

Time ran out.

I won by points. No matter, I won.

An hour or so later, I stood on the first place box and received the gold medal.

My dad still hangs it in his home office.

I looked down at the second and third place winners and shook their hands. They said, "good match." I replied the same and I ran up to my coach who gave me a big hug.

That championship was the highlight of my high school career.

CHAPTER 2

~

Initial Meltdown

Before I left high school and was diagnosed with bipolar disorder, I finally buckled under the pressure. I did something, at least initially, for my father. In the beginning of my junior year, I tried out for the football team.

My sophomore year, I found out I had a passion for football. I immediately wished that I had played my freshman year. I was never truly good, but decent. I managed to make a few key plays throughout the season that helped win games for my team. I also met two of my lifelong friends while I was a part of the football team. One was "Big" Joe. He was always good to me and treated me as an equal even though I was on the JV team and "Big" Joe was on Varsity. The other was a guy named Chris who was the younger brother of one of my teammates. Both would become very important to me in ways I could not have imagined then.

One of our coaches, Coach N, was a former college ball player and resident "tough guy." A mountain of a man, he heavily promoted weightlifting and fitness. His physique suited him because when he was not coaching football, he was the physical education teacher. He also taught geography.

That semester, the first semester of my sophomore year, I was on a medication called Tegretol. I'd been taking that medication since I was in the fourth grade when I suffered a grand mal seizure. Doctors later found these were caused by brain lesions caused by head trauma or injuries I'd had in the past. To keep another grand mal seizure from happening again, I was prescribed Tegretol. This medication would cause me to become deathly sleepy, almost comatose at a certain hour of the day. That hour was, of course, in Coach N's geography class.

The first time he found me, head down and snoozing, Coach N said: "Hines, you fall asleep once more in my class and you'll be standing up on the wall map for the rest of the semester. Got it?"

"It won't happen again," I said.

The next day, I fell fast asleep in the back of the class. I tried to be inconspicuous, leaning on my fist with my arm bent on the desk. Unfortunately, my head fell and slammed on the desk as I simultaneously drooled on my notebook. Coach N acted on the agreement we made the day before. He quietly got the attention of the class, slipped behind me, and yelled at the top of his lungs, "Hines!"

I stood up against the wall-sized map in the back of his room for the rest of the semester. I learned how to sleep standing up with my eyes slightly opened.

It would be a skill I'd put to good use on San Francisco's Muni trains.

The football team's camaraderie was unbreakable to the point of being bulletproof. On the field, we were brothers. Off the field, we protected one another and we were respected. The season ended with six wins and three losses. We even beat the best team in the league, a phenomenal feat for a team that had always been the underdog.

A year later, our high school team went on to the state championship, and I was proud to have been a part of their growth during the prior year. Recovering two fumbles would be my football legacy.

I had to quit the team my junior year due to the erosion of my mental health. This began when my doctor took me off Tegretol after an MRI scan revealed I no longer needed the medication—my brain had healed. My excitement that day was palpable. I was so excited to stop taking that medication. However, that medication is also used to help people who have mental illnesses, acting as an antidepressant and mood stabilizer. Since the fourth grade, it had hindered the development of my manic depression and what would later be diagnosed as bipolar disorder.

When the drug was completely out of my system, I descended into serious psychosis. This scenario was common for those who had taken the same medication in childhood for epilepsy and stopped taking it abruptly. When the year was nearing its end, life quickly unraveled. And it was all due to a white pill—a pill I'd taken since the fourth grade.

When I was a junior in high school, my father filed for divorce and requested an annulment from my mother. The divorce hit me like a ton of bricks. It seemed to affect me much more than it appeared to affect my little brother or older sister.

My father called for a family meeting in the living room. He walked down the stairs and my mother followed, crying. He explained that he was no longer in love with our mom. He told us he had filed for divorce.

I broke down in tears. Libby shrugged as if she had seen it coming. I would later find out that she saw the day approaching for a long time. My brother Joseph was the first to speak. He said in a pragmatic fashion (what would later become a family joke): "So, Dad, do I get to keep the computer?"

It was the only moment that entire day when we laughed together. As a unit and as a tightly knit family, my high school days would be the last time we all laughed together. I would go onto my junior year in 1999 with my dad in the process of divorcing my mom.

My life, I thought, was shattered.

And it was: I would break down that year. I was seventeen and a half years old and I was in for a decade of pain.

That year I was a junior and my drama teacher and mentor cast me to perform the part of Mr. Milton Gatch for the musical, *How to Succeed in Business without Really Trying*. Mr. H was known throughout the city to be a genius when it came to theatrical productions. Though his cast consisted exclusively of high school students, it wasn't unusual for talent scouts to populate the audience, looking for a fresh new acting face.

This wasn't surprising because Mr. H was exceptional at what he did: directing. He could coax the best out of anyone, making sure each and every person shined beneath the pointed glare of the spotlight.

When I first met Mr. H my freshman year we connected in a student-to-teacher way immediately. He was not overtly kind or warm. It was a couple of auditions and two years before my sickness when I stood alone, center stage, and he asked me what part I was auditioning for.

"I'll play a bear skin rug or a lamp post on the stage as long as I get to be a part of this production," I told him. To make my point even more clear, I put a lampshade on top of my head and stood there, waiting for his response.

This must have surprised him. Most other students auditioned not only with a role in mind, but with the intention of making a name for themselves. Two seniors who thought themselves shoe-ins for the part half fumbled lines, boasted aloud, and acted out as if expecting the roles of their choice.

And there I was, proposing to be a lamp. A rug. Maybe he was relieved to see a student who genuinely wanted to be involved for the sake of the production itself. Or maybe he was just amused. Either way, I earned a leading part my sophomore year and Mr. H's attention even though he was known for saying: "I don't give compliments out for nothing."

Which made them all the more prized when he said I did something right.

The two seniors who thought they'd be cast in leading roles stormed the stage and asked Mr. H what he was thinking. It was their senior year, after all. That made them deserve it.

As only Mr. H could, he said: "If you want to be a part of this production, you can. If not, there's the door, don't hit yourself on the way out."

One of them left. He would return days later to accept the menial part in the play.

Mr. H taught me how to memorize lines. I had about three hundred lines for my role in *How to Succeed in Business without Really Trying*.

He told me to read ten lines. Then, repeat those ten lines back to myself, without looking. Read on another ten, and repeat twenty lines back to myself. I would do this until I got through all my lines. By using this method, I ended up knowing every line in the play—another "must-do" according to Mr. H. "That way, you know the movement in a play. Where the characters are going. How the stage is being set." You'd never be lost, in other words, if you knew every single line.

So for that particular production, I did.

When he entered the room, his voice would boom like a highly decorated general, bringing all commotion to an abrupt stop. It was as if that childhood game of freeze was in effect.

Rehearsals required each of us to follow his exact rules—especially no talking when he did. If you did, he'd often say: "Don't second guess me! You'll get your stage time when I give it to you." Or "If I wanted your opinion, I would have asked for it!"

Another pet peeve was walking backward. For some reason, Mr. H had a particular distaste for those who walked opposite the direction they were biologically engineered for. If he caught you walking backward—maybe to reclaim a position if he asked us to go through a particular scene again—he'd put his index finger inside his mouth alongside his cheek and remove it quickly to make a loud, an unbelievably loud, popping sound.

The pop was always loud enough to stop us and make us fall silent even though those of us who'd worked with Mr. H before knew the sound well.

Pop! And then, the inevitable line, directed at whomever had been unfortunate enough to walk backward: "That's the sound of your head coming out of your ass! From the top!"

And from the top, we'd go.

Although Mr. H was a theatrical genius extracting greatness from high school bodies, he was the opposite when it came to himself. A brilliant person on all accounts, he suffered from a behavioral health issue that even I, at such a young age, could see. Usually scathingly sharp and aware of every detail of his production, on performance nights we often saw another side to Mr. H. A side where he was falling over himself. Intoxicated beyond functioning.

I remember the bottle well—parents would bring it to him on performance nights, knowing it was his favorite drink. Even my mom did, once. The tall bottle with the wax seal on it, as though imprinted with a distinction like royalty.

He got drunk at the shows. And though he was the best mentor I've ever had, I could sense, and see, his struggles.

I'll never forget the day Mr. H gave me a compliment.

This was after he told me to quit shooting for roles as the starring lamppost or bear rug. When he said I should practice and work toward a specific role in a specific production.

After all the hints about how to memorize lines and how to move across a stage. Everyone noticed that Mr. H began to pay special attention to me.

Anyway, one day after rehearsal, he came up behind me and said, quickly: "You know, Hines, you could do this for a living. Just saying."

Then he strode off into the darkness behind the curtains of the stage.

Ever since I was about six years old, I wanted to be an actor. I'd sit in front of the bathroom mirror and pretend I was being interviewed by David Letterman—I watched his show as much as I could.

Only, I played the part of both Letterman and the actor. Setting up jokes. Falling for them. Delivering the punch lines. And at age seventeen to hear that I could do that. And that Mr. H said I could.

It was just like my mom and Grandma K said after they watched another performance. "Kevin, you were meant to be on stage."

The only one who disagreed was my dad.

He had a "thing" against celebrities and actors. About how becoming a character on stage could delude a person's sense of self, their sense of right and wrong. If you played too often at inhabiting another reality, who's to say you'd ever come back to the here and now?

He had his reasons for his beliefs. They were grounded in his own interactions with celebrities and actors in years past. He always said he did not have time in his life for artists, those who would inevitably work at their leisure. Yet, it was hard to hear him say: "I despise actors and acting. You should be playing football," on nights he drove me to rehearsals. Acting was something, at the time, I wanted to do. My dad failed to realize the immense work actors do to hone in on a role and perform it to perfection. The greatest actors, the likes of Daniel Day Lewis who just graced *Time* magazine's cover with the bold title as "The Greatest Actor in the World," did not garner such attention for "sitting on their asses painting rainbows." He along with his colleagues in the field of acting or artistry, or filmmaking work diligently and with purpose, just like my father mastered the economy.

Slowly, my father's views have changed over time.

For the time though, acting wasn't meant to be.

I became extremely ill during this time. It was an illness and feeling that I could not describe. I believed people conspired and plotted terrible violence against me, even death. I could be walking anywhere, down the hall, or down a street, and suddenly feel as though I was surrounded by dangerous individuals or groups with evil intentions.

My fellow classmates sensed there was something "off" about me. A trained psychologist would say I had "paranoid tendencies." Paranoia imploded within. One student who knew I was not doing well, and was all for abusing that knowledge, walked by me in the hallway and whispered in my left ear, "Faggot!" The word echoed in my brain. His assumption was that my odd behavior must have been due to my newly founded sexual preference. Although I was not questioning my sexuality, his words in my psychotic brain resonated and twisted my thoughts for a few days.

I felt what it was like to have bipolar disorder for the first time. Of course, then I didn't know that was what was happening to me—that the chemical balance in my brain had tipped too far in one direction. For me, it was as though the reality of the world around me had suddenly shifted.

I had no idea how to keep up with my changing moods or how to cope with a world that was beginning to make less and less sense.

The night before the opening of the play, Mr. H's youngest daughter pushed the answering machine button in their home and a threatening message was heard. A male voice said that if the play did not go well, something terrible would happen to the cast and crew on opening night.

People began to think that because of my paranoid and erratic actions, I was the one who made the call.

I will never forget hearing the words from Mr. H's mouth, the man who said I was meant for the stage. The mentor who had believed in me. He said: "Kevin, if one more person warns me about you—"

This only propelled my paranoia into overdrive. I began to wonder myself, did I do it?

Opening night.

My mom always held parties, inviting friends and family to our house before the opening of any show. It was nice: everyone gathered in our living room and toasted to my forthcoming performance. Then, they would all go to the show and watch me. If I was doing well, I can't tell you how heartwarming it was to gaze out into that darkened audience to see faces I knew, silently cheering me on with their eyes and to see my mother, my biggest acting and performance advocate, smiling back at me.

Shortly before the curtain rose for *How to Succeed in Business without Really Trying*, I succumbed to what can only be described as my first complete and total psychotic break. The paranoia I'd been experiencing over the previous weeks seeped into my soul and saturated it. That night, I began to question the motives of every cast member. I feared that our intermission was going to end in some kind of horrific headline; "School Play Ends in Bloodshed!"

I barely made it through the initial portion of the play before storming off stage mid-sentence. The cast and crew had to quickly recover, filling in the void of silence I'd left.

Mr. H stepped in as my replacement.

He was the only one, besides me, who knew the play's every line.

My mother came to pick me up. She took me home, a place where I could finally feel safe. However, my thoughts were out of control. I could only think of the terrible things other people must be saying about me. It was as if I could hear all of the lies and feel all the hatred in the world—and that it was all focused on *me*. Later, I would come to realize most of it never existed outside my own mind. The group of both cast and crew would dedicate the next few performances to me and my healing.

After that night, I began to see a psychiatrist who prescribed medication to treat my condition. To me, it seemed like I was filling my body with too many contents of bottles—chemicals that were "not me." I felt a shift in my identity; who was this face in the mirror with the contorted expression? When I looked at myself in the mirror, I hated what I saw. When I approached any mirrors in my house, it always felt as if the image I saw was not me but an entirely different person. A person who was out to destroy the person I was. A person who was composed of nothing but rock-hard hate.

He wished awful things on me. I was living a double life, an altered personality. I was never following a strict treatment plan and only appeared to be moving toward wellness.

I remembered a time when, during a psychotic break in my senior year, I threatened to kill one of my good friends. Other memories of that year followed: the mental cloud that kept me focused on my own delusions. The fear that I'd lash out and kill everyone who shared the stage with me for a dramatic production. The way I had come to believe Mr. H didn't believe in me anymore. And then, of course, Mr. H's death.

Depression set in. I said little to those around me about what I was really going through. I would lie about taking my meds, if I took them at all. I also drank copious amounts of alcohol while on antipsychotic medication, something that could prove potentially fatal. When I was home alone on weekends, weekends when my father would travel for work, I sat in my room drinking myself into blackout.

I remember once staying over at my friend Phil's house because I was too drunk to go home.

The night was unforgettable.

We almost burned his house to the ground.

I had left a cartooned t-shirt on a lampshade, with the lamp on all night. Thanks to my asthma, I awoke at the first scent of smoke. Phil was knocked out, dead drunk. I shook him violently to wake him up.

Finally I was able to shake Phil awake and it was in the nick of time. We put out the fire, thanked our good graces and then fell sound asleep.

When we wanted to get drunk, my friends and I would pool our money together and pay an individual on the street to buy us booze. The person would take our money, buy the booze, and get a tip for his service. I occupied this time in my life binge drinking on weekends sometimes with my friends, but mostly alone. It was how I made it through the internal madness.

When I began treatment in 1999, I didn't believe in my heart that I actually possessed this brain disease that the doctors called bipolar disorder. If I had simply taken the advice of my doctors, parents, and nondrinking friends and followed my treatment plan completely, my healing could have been quick and effective. But I denied my symptoms and, consequently, compromised my future.

I managed to barely graduate from high school with straight Cs. I remembered when I had a 2.8, my highest GPA during my sophomore year. An 8 x 10 picture of me went up in one of high school's main upstairs hallways that year for "most improved." It was a proud moment—especially when my parents saw my framed photograph hanging there.

Yet one year later, graduation seemed to be so far from any reality. In 1999 when my GPA reached a low of 2.2, my teachers banded together to place me in the Resource Specialist Program, a scholastic support system for those with learning difficulties. An extremely dismal outlook clouded my vision. During this dark time my mother was my advocate. She became my voice and insisted that I graduate with my class.

Amazingly, in 2000, I was handed my diploma.

It was the same year Mr. H, my mentor of the stage, would lose his life.

Mr. H's death left me utterly collapsed. It sent me back reeling in memories of my senior year, one already marked by turmoil and self-hate. I could have been kicked out of school.

I could still smell his cigarette breath. Even one year later, his senseless and preventable death crushed me. Mr. H had been like an uncle to me. Throughout my high school years, I studied under Mr. H. He was, on first impression, interesting and intriguing. I felt he really understood me.

The man could read people. He was always present. The irony of his passion for perfection and direction on the stage and then his lack of life direction away from it always intrigued me. He also wanted to succeed with his own acting career, and I think he displaced his frustration and anger on his students for not adequately fulfilling his dreams. To say the least, he was a complicated and internally contradicted man with obvious anger issues.

However, I appreciated the fact that he believed in me. We would have powerful conversations about life and how it related to theater, during those few moments we captured together he listened intently. Mr. H could talk about the history of theater or film for days, and not skip a beat. His knowledge of the trade was amazing. He was certainly one of my favorite people on the planet. Sadly he was the first person of so many others that I eventually lost to suicide. He was important to the lives of thousands of high school and college students from San Francisco and the Bay Area and, probably, beyond.

It was June 2000 when Mr. H put a live round in a prop gun and shot himself.

On September 25, 2000, I would jump from the Golden Gate Bridge in an attempt to take my own life.

Before I arrived at the bridge, I saw myself swan diving off the rail, dying and delving deeper into and through the circles of hell to find my mentor. Somehow, I would miraculously bring Mr. H straight up to heaven with me. Inevitably, we would both fight off and battle many demons, possibly Lucifer himself.

I thought of the movie *What Dreams May Come* with Robin Williams. In the film, Williams's character loses both of his children in a terrible car accident. His wife is filled with so much grief that she dies by suicide. Williams's character dies as well and searches for his wife, only to realize that she didn't make it to heaven. I hoped and prayed that I would find Mr. H and have an outcome much like the one in the film. This just goes to show you how very powerful my psychosis was.

I graduated from high school in June 2000, three months before my fall from the bridge.

By the time of Mr. H's death, I had already enrolled at the local college of San Francisco. We called it an extension of high school because it was right across the street.

I remember feeling so inadequate at the time, attending such a "low-level school." My dad wanted me to go to Stanford. He promised me a Ford F-150 quad cab if Stanford accepted me, along with the purchase of a comic bookstore or collection of my dreams. After all, he had gone to University of San Francisco and had graduated with an economics degree. He often told me the story of how, at USF, he enrolled in a Spanish class. To say that he butt heads with his instructor would be a major understatement. My father was considered the class clown.

The instructor reluctantly made a deal with my dad. She said that he could not properly use the word "pretty" to describe a man in the English language. She exclaimed that it was "absolutely impossible." She agreed, however, that if he could pull it off, he would receive an A in the class, no questions asked. He rose from his chair, took a piece of chalk from its tray, peered humorously at his classmates, and wrote, "Dick Butkus [the future Hall of Fame Chicago Bears linebacker in the prime of his legendary career] is *pretty* good at football."

The entire class began to snicker, the snickering turned into laughter, and then it erupted to a roar. The instructor was not amused (to say the least). She took one look at my dad and ordered him out of class, never to return. He was off to the dean's office.

Luckily, my father and the dean were good pals. The dean took my father into his office and said, "We have a problem."

My dad then suggested that the instructor hold up her end of the bargain and give him the A.

The dean made it overwhelmingly clear that it was not in the cards. "You see, she is the head of the language department, and your major is history. You need a language for that major," the dean said.

He had already said no to Italian and no to French; Spanish was his last resort. He asked the dean to plead with the instructor to let him back into the class. The dean tried, but to no avail.

He had to pick another major, on the spot.

The dean brought out the class catalog and together they started looking through it. "What has no language requirement? How about biology?"

"Do I have to dissect stuff?"

"Yes." The dean could tell by the look on my dad's face he was not interested. "Okay, how about art?"

"Are you kiddin' me?"

They moved onto chemistry. My father had already been banned from that major. He may or may not have caused an explosion in the lab.

Then fate paid its visit. They came to the major for whom he was made, as it turns out: economics. My father blurted out, "What's that, like money and stuff?"

"Yes. Money and stuff."

He thought about it for a moment and said, "I like money, I can do that!"

He went on to become a federal banking examiner, helping to take down folks using highly illegal banking tactics. He was then a private banking executive for the next thirty-five years.

In fact, his work in banking necessitated his traveling extensively overseas.

Dad was involved with large companies that have become house-hold names as the banker to some of their main clients where he funded the building of many of their projects such as: the building of oilrigs, railways to new destinations, and buildings in several urban areas across the country. His ability to work with these companies is a testament to his work ethic and his desire to succeed. But nothing demonstrates his unique talents as the brief time when he was involved with a professional hockey team.

In fact, my dad and I always shared our participation in and love of sports. This shared interest would come to full fruition when I was in high school and a member of the wrestling and football teams. How-ever, one sport, hockey, transcended the others and that was a part of our lives without either one of us having to play it (although Dad, when he was younger, did).

By the graces of Dad's successful banking career, he became involved with the Los Angeles Kings. The team was in the red, as they say, and not knowing how to turn loss into profit the then-owners called Dadl.

What I remember of this time is attending nearly all the games. As part owner, Dad secured seats so close to the glass that I could feel the wisps of air that would come off the glass when the players slammed into each other.

Being his son came with perks. I visited the locker room to meet the team players. Once I was given a jersey which all of the players signed. Later, I got a hockey stick, too, with the signatures of the team includ-ing Wayne Gretsky, hockey's greatest. I met him when he played for the Kings. I even appeared on the Jumbotron four square hockey sta-dium video screens for a few minutes while wearing that signed jersey. It was a mock jersey and no one else had it yet!

As I said, Dad was a financial problem-solver and had been awarded great success for his professional abilities. I know he had wanted me to to go to Stanford or some other big-name university; my enrollment at 45 a local college across the street from the high school I had attended was a constant reminder that I was not living up to his expectations of me. He never quite said this, but I have always wanted to make my dad proud of me. And it was then that other reasons beyond my control began to have a negative effect on me.

So, I liked college at first but I could not concentrate. My mental health was rapidly declining. I would have auditory hallucinations during classes and yell out ominous and dark statements like "We are all going to die!" as my head twitched involuntarily from side to side, again and again.

Or, I would scream, "Fuck you, I will kill you!"

Of course I meant myself. The students understood my actions and words differently, though, and many feared for their safety.

CHAPTER 3

~

The Night Before

I was just a kid, only nineteen years old when I jumped from the Golden Gate Bridge. I was, in essence, at the very beginning of my life, yet I could only focus on ending it.

I had given away my most prized possessions, starting with an entire comic book collection worth nearly $5,000, to my younger brother, Joseph, even though I knew he was a notorious creaser of comic books. I had also given away my $400 CD collection to a high school friend. Were I in my right mind, I would have never done that. I even attempted to let go of my grade school and high school trophies, handing them off to friends and acquaintances. My family, friends, or I didn't know that giving away prized possessions in such a hurried manner can exemplify *suicidal ideation*, the idea of suicide takes hold of people and they make plans to kill themselves.

On the night of September 24, 2000, I sat alone in my room, haunted by demons both internal and visible only to me. I had hallucinations of Death himself, hovering above me sickle in hand telling me that I had to come home with him. Giant metallic spiders crawled across my ceiling, down my walls to eat me alive. Above me, the skies opened up and prehistoric dinosaurs flew overhead, screeching as only they can.

I made my plans as a chilling and dangerously demonic voice shouted in my head. The voice was like the one I heard as a boy but never told anyone about. I hid that voice for fear of the outcome. How could I tell those around me that in fourth and fifth grade I heard murmurs in my head, always negative and never fully formed words? As a nineteen-year-old, the appalling voice urged my immediate demise. The voice was loud, the voice was real. *"You are a horrible person! You don't belong here! You have to die, you bastard!"*

I was continuously hammered, browbeaten by this malicious, evil message. Deathly afraid of this alter ego, the bedroom I called my personal space became an awkward, awful place to be—one where my psychosis fed off my insecurities. Daily devouring me, piece by piece.

My bedroom: cold, dark, and lonely.

My room, where a green plastic shell of a Macintosh computer sat on the desk beneath my burgundy and beige bunk bed: places where I had regularly slept and studied. On the far right of my bedroom window was a sticker of Kartman, a character from a favorite television show, the incomparable *South Park*. High school plaques of achievement adorned the walls, ranging from "Most Spirited" to "Most Improved" that I'd earned in both wrestling and football. Stickers from San Francisco radio stations and skateboard clubs lined the large mirror on the white closet door. Pens, printer paper, and drawing pencils lay scattered across my mahogany desk. Carved, plastic framed pictures of my father and I sat on shelves at the back of the desk close to the wall.

Looking into the mirror I recalled the few days I owned and rode a miniature skateboard. I was eight years old. The board's graphics were so cool, a giant leaping lizard, much like the Geico gecko, in an old style body glove–like tank top ran across the bottom of it. I proudly showed it off to all of the neighborhood kids.

My father found me riding it one day. He ripped the board from my hands and snapped it perfectly in half like a twig. I will never forget the noise it made, a loud pop, and the end of a dream. I think he did not want me to become a "skater kid," stereotypically smoking weed all day and continually breaking or fracturing arms or legs.

He broke my heart as he described his action of "trying to protect me."

The quick recollection ended and I headed to the bathroom in a stealthy manner. Staring at myself in the bathroom mirror, as if I were two or three different people, the image whispered to me thoughts of death and self-loathing. This was not the first time. The figure in the mirror was filled with hate, rage, and righteousness. Our awful conversations seemed to go on for an hour. Clearly this terrible version of me wanted nothing but my undoing, repeating declarations like, *"No matter what you do, you cannot escape me. You will die by my hands. It is inevitable, the choice is not your own."*

Walking back from the bathroom to my bedroom, I glared at a poster of my favorite pro wrestler, Dwayne "The Rock" Johnson. I greatly admired the Rock like so many of my high school classmates did. Hell, I worshiped the guy, imitating him for years. Months prior to my darkest day, my father had come home from a business trip with an autographed copy of his picture. I had always wanted to be as confident, entertaining, and as powerful a presence.

That night, looking at the poster I felt powerless, inadequate, and helpless, like a complete failure. The Rock was a champion, hugely successful and at the time, my idol.

What was I, compared to him?

I was a disturbed young man unable to control my emotional and mental state or physical actions.

I was alone, how could I ever achieve anything?

These thoughts and feelings and questions tormented me. The misguided answers my sick brain gave me only solidified the belief that I had to die.

A couple of days before these mentally unstable revelations came to me, a mosquito had bitten me. My severe psychosis led me to the horrifying thought that I might have AIDS. I came up with a ridiculous solution to kill the "virus." I took a can of Lysol and sprayed myself with it, top to bottom, and then sprayed and drenched my bedsheets. I did not realize the consequence of my actions or that I was continuously inhaling these fumes that soon made me dizzy. I couldn't comprehend the toxicity of those chemicals.

I'd stopped sleeping regularly. In the previous fourteen days, I had slept perhaps a total of six hours. I would try to sleep, but I kept coughing from the fumes. As I inhaled, the room spun out of control, shadows of darkness filled the ceiling, and shape-shifting demons contorted the space. Red eyes glowed above me and claws clutched at me, tearing my body apart.

Was this all in my mind?

It felt real.

It tasted real.

I could smell it and I could hear it.

I heard the vicious voice say: *I had to take my life!*

There was no other option.

I powered up my computer and searched online for my only solution. I found a website that *recommended* I kill myself. This site was one of many that promoted suicide. These people are intrinsically connected to deaths all over the world and nearly became connected to mine.

This particular site told me that because I live in San Francisco, I had an easy, foolproof way to die. I read these words: "There is no chance you will live. Go the Golden Gate Bridge and jump off. You will die on impact, Good Luck!"

I swallowed this miserable message whole. I had *tunnel vision* (another term used by suicidologists—the doctors and clinicians who dedicate their lives to prevention of suicide). My focus within this tunnel vision was narrow.

There was only one way out.

No other thought occurred to me; certainly not the tremendous consequences of my actions. Only those demons haunting my every waking moment, haunting my dreams were real. When I got a bit of sleep, I would be awakened with night terrors.

This horrific suicidal thought shamed me down to the bone. Discrimination is attached to people who think about, talk about, or attempt suicide. I could not tell a soul of my true thoughts. The tunnel was now pitch black. Never knowing of anyone to survive, I was ready to take this irreversible action.

What I failed to see was that, by ending my life, I would cause interminable pain to my family and friends. I could not understand the heartbreak it would cause those around me. Nor did I consider that my brother, Joseph, might live the rest of his life in continual rage, or that my sister Libby might shut herself off from the world and fall into perpetual depression, silence, and sadness mistakenly blaming themselves for my death as many family members do when they lose someone they love to suicide. I certainly held no understanding of the enormous pain my mother and father would suffer because they lost their oldest son in such a terrifying and devastating way. They would not have a chance to watch me mature, marry, and perhaps have children. Instead, all of their hopes, aspirations, and dreams for me would be destroyed with my decision to end my life by jumping off the Golden Gate Bridge.

The brain disease I had developed, bipolar disorder, results from an imbalance of chemicals in the brain. The imbalance affects the way a person thinks, acts, and feels. Rapid cycling, psychotic features characterize the type of bipolar disorder from which I suffer. Subsequently, I have manic highs, extreme paranoia, auditory and visual hallucinations, grandiose thoughts, panic attacks, and depressive lows.

Because of these extreme symptoms, I had battled for two years and I thought I could battle no longer.

It was impossible to think about brighter days.

My brain was unable to feed me positive thoughts or affirmations.

I was disturbed, in the deep and darkest pits of psychosis. The voices beckoned once more, "How would or could *I* ever achieve anything?" The only answer that came to mind was, *"You can't and you won't. You are completely useless, and a burden to all!"* This answer kept me from asking anyone for help.

That evening, while I paced in my room finalizing the planning process of how to end it all, my father talked on the phone with my psychiatrist. They discussed my erratic behavior over the last few weeks for more than two and a half hours.

The doctor was reassuring my dad and said these exact words: "It's just another episode. He'll come out of it in a couple of days. Don't worry about a thing."

Even today, my father's biggest regret was not taking me to a hospital that night.

My parents trusted the doctor and relied on his expert opinion. His advice seemed reasonable. We were unaware that the doctor was addicted to methamphetamines the entire time he treated me and his other patients.

I remember him as a tall pudgy white man who was always pushing his rimmed glasses up his nose. He was quiet, almost feeble, yet kind, and even a bit delicate. The majority of my other experiences with clinicians in the field of mental health have been uplifting, empowering, and life-altering. This one, however, was tragic. His story would end badly; after his scandal was revealed, he lost his license to practice. Years after that, he died of a drug overdose.

I focused for a few moments after slipping further and further away from reality to write my suicide note. I rejected draft after draft. I did not like how hateful I sounded with each letter. I expressed so much anger toward my family and friends. They deserved none of this vitriol, but with so much anger eating me up, I lashed out by projecting it on them.

Later, we could not find all of these drafts. I vaguely remember hiding all of them in a brown paper bag and stuffing the bag at the bottom of the recycling bin. It took between five and eight drafts to finally write a version I "liked."

Yet, I know I may have hallucinated that entire experience. I may have only written one note or I may have written many. I remember the final copy of my final suicide note reading something like this:

Dear Mom, Dad, Libby, Joseph, Family and Friends,

I can no longer take living and I hate myself. I am so sorry, but I cannot be here anymore. Mom, you're not always right, so don't think you are, but I love you. Dad, yelling doesn't help anyone. Stop being so mean-spirited, but I love you. Joseph, keep up the DJ stuff, someday you'll be a household name. Libby, some day you'll be a world-renowned film director; good luck. To my girlfriend: This is not because of you, it is because of me. To my best friend, you'll find a new friend. Thank you for always being there for me.

Please forgive me

To quiet my mind I began pacing back and forth in my bedroom, counting down the hours until I could go to the bridge and finally end the pain.

This is no cliché.

It was how I felt.

People who attempt or die by suicide need that same outcome: feeling as though the immeasurable pain must end, regardless of the means to end it.

Everyone else in the house was asleep. Quietly, I went into the bathroom to talk with my reflection one more time. I stared into the bathroom mirror at what was a complete stranger. I saw two people standing face to face and separated by one shiny piece of reflective glass. I did not see myself, but rather, a hardened suicidal maniac.

The stranger mouthed to me in another eerie death whisper, *"You're a dead man! I hate you! You have no choice, I will kill you! If not today then eventually, I promise you—this is inevitable! You must die! You must die!"*

I began to cry and whispered, *"I don't want to die. I am a good person. Please don't kill me."*

In response, "he" punched the mirror until it cracked from corner to corner.

This battle lasted another hour.

I stumbled back to my room. Around 5:00 a.m., after one more review, I placed my suicide note into my notebook and put the notebook into my black book bag that I used for college. I did not want the bag to be too heavy, so I left all of my textbooks on my desk.

At 6:00 a.m., I went to my father's room. My dad slept with an apparatus, a loud Darth Vader–like mask and machine. I often imagined him speaking with it attached to his mouth, "Kevin, I am your father!"

He was sound asleep and quite startled when I woke him.

"Jesus, Kev, what time is it?"

"It's six."

"Kev, I don't have be at work until 9:00. Is everything OK?"

"Yes, Dad, everything's fine, I just wanted to say good morning."

"Go back to bed! I'll see you when I'm up." He rolled over.

I left the room thirty minutes later after sitting cross-legged and in silence by his bedside. I was in a fury of mental anguish. Sitting there, tears ran down my face as my body involuntarily rocked back and forth. The pain had to stop, at any cost.

At 7:00 a.m., he came into my room with a worried look on his face. "Are you OK? Do we need to go to your doctor today?"

A logical question from the pragmatic realist that he is, it was a great question. Here was my opportunity to reach out and grab the help that I desperately needed. But instead, for the next fifteen minutes, I pretended to be all right, lying to convince my father that everything was fine.

I played the role of someone happy and well before the curtain fell and I could return to my state of misery. By then, I was swept up by another common emotion of those who become suicidal and have almost reached the point of an attempt. A form of manic *elation* emerged and I was finally ridding myself of this monstrous, epic pain.

I was going to be free!

No more night terrors. No more hallucinations of the grim reaper coming to my room with his staff and blade to take me away. No more twisting stomach cramps from the stress of this brain disease. Freedom was in sight and only a direct question (Are you thinking of harming yourself?) could stop me now.

In my mind, dying meant I would either be home in the euphoria of heaven, held up by God's hand or damned forever in the molten lava like ten circles of hell. My Catholic background painted a pretty clear picture for me.

As I neared the attempt, my faith all but disappeared.

Plus, my dad was not completely convinced by my attempt to act like everything was OK. "Why don't you come to work with me, Kevin? Or we could go to the beach? No, what if we go see a movie? We can do whatever you want. I just want you to be near me today."

His fatherly instincts were spot-on, but I persisted. Everything was OK.

I told him that I had a math test and tons of work that I couldn't miss.

More lies.

He'd forgotten that I would not willingly take a math test if someone had paid me. Mathematics had always been my worst subject. After listening to my mountain of excuses, Dad finally and reluctantly bought my act.

He said that he'd give me a lift to college. I told my dad that after classes, I could take the bus home since college was less than a block away.

He, feeling more at ease, jumped at the idea. "That would be perfect, Kev, I will see you back home at 5 or 6 p.m."

During the drive, Dad asked again about how I was doing. Still, I pretended everything was hunky-dory. The whole time, I was worried that he could read my mind and that he would surely find me out. I believed that he'd lock me up in the state hospital.

I was more eager to die than to deal with proper treatment in a psychiatric hospital. I was convinced that if anyone knew of my suicide plan, I'd be locked up for good—the vision of white walls and being fastened into a straitjacket—to never be seen or heard from again.

Dad dropped me off at college, right across from my old high school. I kissed my father on the cheek good-bye. I had done this my entire life, and he had done this to his father and I imagine his father to *his* father. Sometimes, it reminded me of some sort of Hollywood mafia film scenario. My father is an old school San Franciscan; his personality reminds me of the epitome of a movie mafia character. If you knew him or my late Great Uncle Kevin for less than five seconds you would completely understand.

"I love you, Kevin," he said. "Be careful."

Dad has said this since I was a little kid, and he continues to say it to this day. He will most likely say these words until the day I die—of natural causes.

"I love you, too, Dad."

I watched my Dad drive off in his hard-earned forest green, beige leather, and wood interior Vanden Plas Jaguar. I thought, *this is the last time I will ever see anyone I love, and the very last time anyone I love will see me.*

A tear streamed from my right eye and slowly rolled down my cheek. It reached my jaw and was heavy enough to drop off my face and onto the lace of my right shoe. I think of that moment often, especially when I am having a bad mental health day. It was that moment I knew I was finished with this earth.

CHAPTER 4

~

The Bridge

Life can be pretty complex; details are important to paint the perfect picture.

I wore my favorite outfit right out of the 1990s, simple and monochromatic, beige from head to toe. I wore a light beige ribbed, form-fitting V-necked sweater, a pair of light beige cargo pants, with what seemed like 300 pockets, and a pair of dark beige Lugz shoes with white rubber soles. I wore the ensemble with the gold chain that my mother had given me for my high school graduation. I still have that gold chain. It now sits in the valet where I keep my watches, pins, cufflinks, extra buttons, keys, and collar stays.

My plan proceeded.

As I entered the campus, I figured that I should tie up loose ends. I walked to the counselor's department, into a female counselor's office and requested that she drop nine and a half of my twelve and a half units, leaving me with just one class, English. I did not want my family to have to deal with that nuisance after my death.

Without question, hesitation, or thought she dropped the courses and I was on my way. What she should have done was inquire as to why I needed to drop the majority of my units immediately; she should have asked if everything was OK.

That day, I attended that final English class.

It was my favorite class, and in it my favorite teacher. My preference had little to do with the subject. I was certainly not a literary master. The reason was simple, the teacher, Mrs. K, was smoking hot.

I arrived to class about twenty minutes late and she scolded me. I was paranoid and thought that someone would find me out and thwart my plan. I reached into my bag, pulled out my suicide note and signed it:

Sincerely, Kevin Hines,

I left class early. Once more, Mrs. K was fuming. Yet, I didn't stick around to apologize or mull over her annoyance. As planned, I left campus.

It was not quite 10:00 a.m. The weather was overcast with patches of moist, low-density fog lying above every street as it often is in San Francisco. I knew the fog would probably burn off later in the day, and I would not live to see the sun glinting through the gray.

I walked briskly toward the Municipal railway stop on Ocean Avenue. The city was bustling with people from the community college, a nearby gas station, those running in and out of fast-food restaurants, across and down the street, and the Muni bus terminal I was standing in.

Thinking of nothing else but death, I stepped onto the concrete island and looked for the bus. In answer to my need to get to the bridge as fast as humanly possible, a K train swiftly arrived.

I felt slightly elated: No one had found me out. No one had a clue. I brought just enough money to ride the bus, transfer to another bus, and take the next bus to the bridge. My head was in a daze, my mind began to wander; my thoughts were all over the place.

When I got off the K to transfer to the next bus, I was hungry. I quietly muttered to myself, "I better eat before I die. Yeah, I need a last meal." I would have enjoyed a large steak and potato plate with a side of A.1. sauce but I didn't have any money and the steak and potato joint in view was closed in the morning. Instead, I walked to the drugstore and went straight to the candy aisle. I quickly pocketed a pack of Starbursts and my favorite Wild Berry Skittles.

After completing my five-finger discount, I walked the two blocks to the next bus stop. This bus went directly to the Golden Gate Bridge parking lot. For me this was the bus's last stop. I got on the bus and sat in the very back, in the middle of the last seat. Sitting alone, I ate my "last meal."

My heart pounded.

It seemed ready to jump out of my chest.

My eyes were wide.

My thoughts raced as my adrenaline levels were off the charts. Any good psychologist would have noticed my misery, but there wasn't a mental health professional in sight.

I began to cry softly to myself. Tears soon poured down my face. I was like a frightened newborn just entering into the world, alone, naked, and vulnerable. I could see people on the bus glancing at me, and then they began to stare. Their looks felt piercing and incriminating, which worsened my delusions. In my head, I heard those appalling voices, urging self-destruction. The voices were determined, purposeful, and screaming at me, "*You are a horrible person, die now, you must die!*" Such self-hatred, such inner turmoil was unbearable.

One of the voices crushed the others, became my only adversary. He wanted my soul. His words, my words, were crystal clear: "*You are a burden to your family. You do not deserve to live! Die now! Jump now! Do it! I hate you! I will kill you!*"

Even in the face of such daunting voices, my ambivalence grew. I was wavering between believing I had to die and desperately wanting to live. I had no idea that this kind of reaction is quite common for someone contemplating suicide, especially someone with serious mental health issues. Dying, which had seemed so certain and obvious, now terrified me. A part of me was frantically trying to convince myself that I indeed did deserve to live. A part of me pleaded with that "other" self to carry on and find help.

In all honesty I, Kevin Hines, never wanted to die. It was not my rational, conscious choice or decision. I *believed* I had to. Compelled by my bipolar disorder, my brain illness, I was to complete this terrible act.

The bus approached the bridge, pulled into the parking lot. I started to comprehend the scope of my intention, the scale of my actions: *Today was going to be the very last day of my life*.

Suddenly, my viewpoint changed. Earlier, I had feared that my father or someone at school would discover my plan.

Now I wanted nothing more than to be found out.

With all of the people on that bus, I wanted one of them to read my mind. I wanted someone to sense my despair. My eyes flickered from person to person. I hoped that one of them would sense my pain and my need for recognition. I contracted a pact with myself: if someone asked me, "Hey kid, are you OK? Is something wrong?" or "Can I help you?" I would tell them everything. The only question that remained was: Would someone have listened to me?

Would a stranger on that bus have helped me?

Would you?

One big problem with the pact I made was: not one person who saw me on that bus crying my eyes out asked me anything at all.

People stared but did not intervene. They may have wondered but never asked, adhering to the old adage "It's not my problem." Or "It's none of my business."

After we pulled up to the Golden Gate Bridge stop, I thought I had found help in the bus driver. Everyone stepped off the bus. I was the last off.

I walked slowly toward the driver.

When I had almost reached him, he said, "Come on kid, get off the bus, I got to go!"

This was not quite the intervention for which I had been praying.

I wiped the tears from my face. Many more replaced them. A flurry of tears fell. Inside, I was hysterical. On the outside, I was holding it together until the bitter end, behavior all too common for suicidal individuals who tend to make some kind of inner pact that lets us back out from the worst decision of our lives.

As I stepped from the bus and into the cold, damp morning, the now singular voice in my head screamed at its loudest. It was overwhelming. Again and again, it said, *"You must die! You must die! Jump now! You don't have a choice! Die!"*

Have you ever been to the Golden Gate Bridge? If not, you may have seen pictures. The view and bridge are incredibly beautiful. A roadway is designated for cars, and sidewalks line the east and west of the bridge for walkers, runners, and cyclists. A handrail and a small ledge are on the other side of the railing—the sort of ledge found in the movies, where a jumper will perch while the authorities talk him down from the end. The Golden Gate Bridge does not have netting or barriers to keep anyone from leaping off. The bridge provides no safety for those suffering from mental afflictions, drug-induced, or otherwise. I believe no one really wants to die from jumping off any structure. For those who die this way, I wholeheartedly believe they feel they have no other choice, as I did.

Amid this beautiful setting, I paced back and forth, up and down the walkway for half an hour, trying to talk myself out of my brain's decision. I stumbled along, my breath rapid, my heart hammering as though it were to soon blast through my ribcage. The relentless voice still demanded, with rage, "*You must die! Jump now! There are no alternatives!*"

My eyes were red, tear-filled, and swollen. Soon after I had picked "The Spot," a woman approached me.

She was ravishing!

Angelic.

I knew it. *This was what I had been waiting for.* This was the woman who was going to save my life. She was going to ask me if I was OK.

I didn't have to die.

She wore giant Chanel-looking sunglasses, the kind a Hollywood star would wear, the kind women everywhere who dare to be fashionable wear, the kind of sunglasses that don't fit faces.

She came up to me, smiling from ear to ear. In what sounded like an Eastern European accent, she asked, "Vil you take my picture?"

My heart sank, and then *crumbled.* I had thought she was going to be my salvation! How could she not see that I was in tears, in obvious pain?

How could she not want to save me?

I took her picture several times as she altered her position for each shot. She smiled for the camera as I snapped several photographic souvenirs of her visit as tears streamed down my face and my heart sank lower than I thought it could.

She thanked me, turned her back, and walked away. That was it.

I muttered my last thought before the jump to myself: "Nobody cares! Absolutely nobody cares."

Of course, in reality, everyone cared: my family, friends, and people to whom I had not with spoken in five years. They all cared.

I walked back toward the traffic railing. As if nothing else mattered, I ran, channeling an Olympic hurdler, striding light, fast and determined.

I used my arms to catapult myself over the rail.

I did not get on the ledge to be talked down. I jumped quickly, without recourse, falling head first, fast and hard into the wind and empty space below me.

I reached back for the rail. It wasn't there.

In the midst of my free fall, I said to myself these words, words I thought no one would ever hear me repeat: *"What have I done? I don't want to die. God, please save me!"*

CHAPTER 5

∼

The Miracle

I fell at a speed of seventy-five miles per hour.

The end was imminent.

The drop is estimated at 220 feet, or twenty-five stories. This is two-thirds the height of San Francisco's world famous Transamerica Pyramid building. My skin felt as if the rough winds would literally tear through it with like tiny needle-sized shards of glass, digging into my hands, my face, and neck. Rapidly falling head first, toward the choppy, green sea, I felt an immense rush, unmatched by any experience I have ever had.

Instinctively, I knew that if I landed as I was—head first—I would die. I would be killed outright or break my neck, become paralyzed, and drown. My only hope was to land feet first. As I fell at seventy-five miles per hour, I somehow possessed the mind-set that *all I wanted to do was live*—by any means necessary.

I threw my head back and uttered one mighty prayer: "God, please, please let me live! Heaven save me!" Perhaps it was the force of my head being thrown back or maybe another powerful gust of wind. Perhaps it was a nudge from my guardian angel, or Jesus Christ Himself who turned my body around, because I hit the water feet first, in a sitting position. I learned later that it is one, if not the only, way to survive such a fall.

The impact was like hitting a brick wall at seventy-five miles an hour in my dad's Jaguar.

The impact reverberated through my toes, went up through my legs, and into my torso. My two lower vertebrae, T-12 and L-1, shattered and splintered like glass piercing my lower organs. By some miracle, the shards missed my heart and my lungs.

There are no words for the pain.

It was unimaginable.

The night before, I read that I would die upon impact. I did not know that I would be the twenty-sixth person to survive from a list of over two thousand who had permanently made their exits into the afterlife by jumping off the Golden Gate Bridge in San Francisco, the beloved City by the Bay. On average, two people leap from the bridge every ten days. This has been relatively consistent since the bridge's completion in 1937. Unfortunately, these depressed and troubled men and women quickly die by suicide from the readily accessible railing of the Golden Gate Bridge. I can't claim to know why they jumped to their deaths, but I would wager a guess that I relate to what drove them more than most.

On the bridge above, horrified people leaned over the rail. They couldn't have seen the impact my body felt as it slammed to a complete halt. To them it looked as if I quickly disappeared into the abyss.

Yet, that crashing stop created all of the internal damage I sustained. Then, a rippling vacuum pulled me deep under the water.

What happened next? I opened my eyes. I was alive. I was in excruciating pain, but I was still here.

The water was dark green and murky.

I did not know which way was up or down.

My legs were utterly useless, immobile. In a panic, I began swimming using only my arms. The water got darker and colder.

Oh, shit! I was swimming in the wrong direction, toward the bottom of the bay. My ears rang; my head throbbed. I was running out of air. My eyes felt as though they were bulging out of my head. I felt the extreme cold of the water seep into my body. I writhed, wondering: Could I even make it to the surface?

This was not the plan. I cannot drown. I do not want to drown! I pulled myself with my arms using all my strength. I began to see the glimmer of the surface. It was so far and I couldn't seem to swim fast enough.

I had reached complete exhaustion but I kept on going, moving my arms. The glimmer above me began to lighten.

I would not give up. I had to live.

My eyes felt like they were popping out of my head, due to the lack of oxygen. Each stroke took tremendous effort that left a wake of burning in my shoulders and back. I felt that I was going to pass out and drown. *No!* I told myself.

Just one last stroke, you can do this! No, not this way, God, not like this, I don't want to drown, please save me. I made a mistake.

I broke the surface.

I attempted to take a giant gasp of that cold air around my face. All I could manage was a silent yelp, like that of an infant. *Please let this all be a nightmare or another hallucination!*

I was supposed to die on impact. Isn't that what the website promised?

Horrendous pain gripped me as I bobbed up and down on the surface of the water, treading water with my arms. Pain stabbed my back, and my lower abdomen felt as if it had imploded.

I could not draw a deep breath. *But the voices now good or bad were gone.* They were gone! All thoughts of suicide were erased from my mind, gone without a trace. *Not today. I can't die now! I must do everything I can to survive.*

September 25, 2000, would not be the day I died by suicide.

This would instead be the day of my awakening. No matter how often I thought of death by my hands, I would never die this way.

Something else more profound occurred after I broke the surface. My faith in God returned—with force. After my mental breakdown and up until the moment I jumped, I had questioned the existence of a higher power.

Not anymore. I felt God's presence. He cradled me. He bobbed in the water with me. When I could no longer move or fight to live, He guided me. He must have adjusted my position in the air. He must have carried me down into the water and back to the surface.

Only He could have given me the instinct to resist death and struggle to stay above water, to stay alive.

I treaded water. Painfully, I turned my wrenched neck to the right. I saw a cement pillar twenty-five yards away; a ladder attached to it. If

I could get to it, I could hold on until someone rescued me. I tried to swim as fast as I could, but I had to pull up my whole body using only my arms. From the moment I hit the water my legs had stopped moving. I swam, and swam, and swam only to find out I had not altered my position an inch. The pillar at this point seemed unattainable.

To my left, about twenty-five to thirty yards away, a red and white metal buoy bobbed atop the extremely frigid water. If I could reach it, I could hang on and pray that someone would pull me out.

Again, although I thought I was making progress, I hardly moved a centimeter. The currents were too strong.

Some days, as many as six currents move in different directions simultaneously under that part of the bridge. Between my exhaustion, pain and inability to kick, I was no match for the choppy waters of the San Francisco Bay.

I was having trouble staying afloat. Physical and mental lethargy had set in. Then something hit me. Something bumped into my torso and started swiftly circling beneath me. I reached out to it with an outstretched hand. It felt very slimy.

My first thought was that a great white shark had sensed my weakness and had come to devour me. I was more fearful than ever. But this creature didn't take a huge chunk out of me.

Instead, it *helped* me, circling beneath me bumping me up.

I was no longer treading water. I was floating—floating on top of it! However, I worried that this unseen creature might eventually attack me or was poising to do so and simply taking its time. With my good arm, I began to punch into the water, hoping to scare the thing away.

It never wavered. Nor did it bite me. Later, I found out it was a sea lion.

Years later, a man who was on the bridge and less than two feet away from me when I jumped, told me he saw the sea lion swimming and circling underneath me.

He had taken pictures of me as I lay above the water while the sea lion bumped me up. It was a morbid but amazing scene. When we spoke after a media appearance, he told me about the pictures. Apparently, if a sea lion sees or senses something in danger, it often tries to help, much like dolphins have done all around the world. I consider this piece of my story nothing short of a major miracle.

People have contradicted my story, saying that this portion of the event was a figment of my imagination, or a complete hallucination. Believe what you will, I was there.

Even my mother continues to question the part about the sea lion. I have the direct e-mail to ABC TV from the man who took pictures that day from the bridge. I have my memories of that day, too. Of a creature holding me up when my legs were too injured to do the job themselves. Witnesses from that day stood on that bridge on September 25, 2000, and happened to see a nineteen-year-old wearing only beige attempt to take his life and fail. Instead, he was saved by a miracle. And a sea lion.

The sea lion did not leave from beneath me until I heard the humming of a boat racing toward me. The Coast Guard arrived right before hypothermia set in, sparing me death, either in the water or soon thereafter in the hospital.

The only reason the Coast Guard reached me as fast as they did was because a woman driving on the bridge saw me jump. She had a car phone and she called a friend who also happened to be a member of the Coast Guard.

By then, I was too exhausted to hold my neck up, so my head fell back in the water. I prayed that the boat's propeller would not sever a limb, or for that matter, my head.

The boat pulled up right next to me.

The mammal beneath me zoomed off.

"Stay right there. Don't move!" someone shouted. Two men jumped in the water, gripped me, and hoisted me up.

Quickly, they grabbed my forearms in a crisscrossed manner and maneuvered me onto a flat white board. They cut through my soaked sweater to check for any visible damage or internal hemorrhaging. They could not wait for proper techniques and check for injuries.

One officer said: "Hey, kid, do you know what you just did?"

"Yes, I just jumped off of the Golden Gate Bridge."

"Why did you do that?"

My pathetic answer was, "I don't know, I guess I had to die."

The officer replied, "Do you know how many people we pull out of this water already dead?"

The other officer had a different approach. He put his hand on my head and said, "You're a miracle, kid." Then he asked, "Who are your parents and how do we reach them?"

The Coast Guard vessel reached headquarters, where they transported me from their boat into a waiting ambulance.

The ride to the hospital was riddled with agony. I was still dealing with the same asthma attack. I feared death's doors were opening. I asked for an inhaler to abate the asthma attack and breathe easier, but the paramedics could not give me one because they did not know how or if my lungs had been impacted by the fall. Oxygen was all that I received.

We arrived at the hospital's emergency entrance and everyone who rushed to treat me seemed to be in a panicked state. It was almost like an engrossing television episode of E.R.

Time was of the essence.

I had survived the jump.

But I might not survive my injuries.

I might not survive the night.

At the time of the jump, my mother was at a nurses's seminar on depression. She was proactively working on empathizing with and understanding my disorder. When she received the call from the Coast Guard, she was devastated to learn what I had done.

My father got the news in a blunt and overwhelming way. The woman who called him from the hospital did not ask, "Are you sitting down?" Or say: "I have some difficult news." None of that. When my dad answered the phone the private bank where he worked, he heard, "Mr. Hines, your son has just jumped off the Golden Gate Bridge."

Stunned, my father said only three words. "Is he alive?"

"Yes, he is alive."

My father did not believe her at all. He is a fourth generation San Franciscan and he knew what jumping off the Golden Gate Bridge meant. He assumed that she was simply avoiding the truth, waiting until he arrived at the hospital—where he would view me in a body bag and be asked to identify his eldest son.

His next thought was simple: he did not want to crash his car on the way to the hospital, he asked his secretary to ride in the car with him.

"Why?" she asked.

"So I don't drive off a cliff on the way to the hospital. My son has just jumped off of the Golden Gate Bridge." His secretary deserves a badge of honor for getting in the car at all.

I don't remember who entered my room first, but one entrance remains stuck in my mind. This was the most gut-wrenching moment of my time in the trauma center.

I was conscious and hooked up to all kinds of hospital hardware that dripped fluid into my arms and that beeped at a regular cadence. My dad, whose friends call him "Big Patty," is a man I had never seen cry, not for a death in the family, not for anything. He was usually as stoic as a rock; most who know Dad consider him a tough son of a bitch.

He took one look at me and began to sob, replicating the outpour of my tears when I was on the bridge. He had never cried in front of me. When I saw his tears and heard his words, "Kevin, I am sorry," my own eyes began to water.

My father's immediate reaction was guilt, guilt he nor anyone I know or love should have harbored. When these occurrences happen one million times around the world every year, guilt and the blame game should never, not ever be placed on anyone's shoulders. That kind of guilt is far too much to bear.

"No, Dad, I am sorry," I said.

He came over to the left side of my hospital bed. He put his hand on my forehead and kissed me on the top of my head. "You are going to be okay. You'll make it through this, I promise." When he said those words, I knew I would be OK. I knew I would make it through this the worst chapter in my life, one of the worst events in our family's history.

When my mother arrived, she said: "Well, I guess God wants you to win that Oscar."

That put an immediate smile on my face. Her optimism always did.

These were much-needed words from both my mother and father. I fiercely wanted to live. I needed to live. I was not finished with this life and I prayed that I would be granted a coveted second chance.

After all of the mental anguish that had led to my jump, I finally felt hope. Ironically, I saw my future even though I was severely injured and momentarily without the use of my legs.

The doctors told my father that I only had a 50 percent chance of living through the night. I had half a chance, but other odds were stacked against me.

My estimation is that more than 2,000 people have jumped from the Golden Gate Bridge to their deaths. As of 2012, the former coroner and friend of mine had proven that there were 1,558 confirmed deaths off the Golden Gate Bridge. The unaccounted for have either been washed away to sea, eaten by fish, or have been considered "accidental deaths."

In seventy-five years of the bridge's existence, only thirty-three have survived the fall. I was number twenty-six.

That's a survival rate of 0.002 percent. Only a fraction of these people fully recover from their injuries. Many have already died of natural causes, and only one who survived went back to the bridge and ended his life there.

Of the survivors, nineteen of them have come forward and expressed words to this effect: "The second my hands and feet left the rail I realized I had made a mistake," "I realized how much I needed to live," or "I didn't want to die."

The doctors could not predict whether I would recover or I would die. I had considerable injuries to address before I could become a member of "The World's Most Exclusive Survivors's Club."

My back had been crushed.

The splinters of two shattered vertebrae lacerated the organs in my abdomen. The doctors kept my pain down with high doses of morphine.

Another miracle saved me. A specialist in injuries to the spine just happened to be at the hospital that day. He had been at the hospital on a particular assignment and had planned to leave a day or so before I arrived. For some reason, he stayed longer.

Fortunately, he was there when I arrived since the extent of my injuries required an operation. Once again, I knew fate was on my side. The doctor explained the recommended surgery to my parents. The surgery would last eight to twelve hours. My parents agreed. In essence, they had no choice than to sign on the dotted line.

The doctor began the surgery with an incision through my left side. He and his team pulled out my intestines, stomach, and other organs. They laid them on my chest and went to work:

They successfully removed all of the shattered pieces of my T-12 and L-1 and L-2 vertebrae.

They sutured up my lacerated organs.

They removed a three-inch piece of my tenth rib from my left side.

They made a paste from the rib piece and the shards of vertebrae.

They placed the paste into a cylindrical titanium cage and put the cage around the area of the missing vertebrae.

When they finished, they took four surgical screws and fitted a metal plate to the left side of the cage to hold the metal fixture in place. The repaired vertebrae and part of the left tenth rib were fused together so that I would be able to walk again.

While under anesthesia, I suffered another violent asthma attack— while the surgeon's scalpel was still in my body! Mercifully, no further damage was done.

They finished the surgery by piecing me back together with twenty-three staples across the side of my torso.

The scar isn't pretty and will never go away. The scar is a reminder of harder times, but keeps me in the here and now. When I become suicidal today I need only look at it in the mirror and be thankful to still be around.

After all: I survived.

Then as now: being alive is all that matters.

Days later as I lay in a hospital bed recovering from my injuries, another suicide attempt survivor of Golden Gate Bridge was rolled into the room with me.

The medical staff asked me to help identify the young man. They thought it was my best friend. As it turned out, the two of us who had survived the fall one right after the other had never met.

During my trauma center stay, the surgeon, his team, and the nursing staff not only worked around the clock to keep me breathing, they repaired my spine and gave me back use of my legs. Considering the devastating damage I had done to my body, I healed relatively quickly.

Ironically, during my hospital stay, I feared every day that I might die from complications of the surgery. My friends and immediate and extended family all shared that worry. My father, in particular, asked the doctors if there was anything he could do. Doctors lightened his worries by reassuring him that the medical team was doing everything possible to keep me alive. The staff also told my parents that they believed I would *live*, but how much I would recover was yet to be determined.

The hospital's chaplain, a Franciscan Friar named Brother Daniel Harper, visited me. His first question to me was, "What are you in for kid?"

"I jumped off of the Golden Gate Bridge."

"Yeah, and I'm the Pope!"

I guess he hadn't heard this one.

After we clarified fact from fiction, he visited me every day.

Each time, he would place his right hand on my forehead, hold his rosary in his left hand, and pray. When he was done, he would always say, "Kevin, when you feel better, you must talk about this. Your story can help people."

I didn't believe him. My answer was always the same: "No, Brother Daniel, I am too ashamed."

I thought he was out of his mind.

How could I help people?

But every time he saw me, he reminded me of what became my calling. He was the first to tell me that my story could save lives. At the time, I did not know that he was the president of the San Francisco Suicide Prevention Board. Little did I know, he had a plan for my future.

I was also touched by everyone's reactions when the news got around about my attempted suicide, miraculous survival, and intended recovery. My closest friends flooded the hospital's waiting room, hoping to see me.

Initially, they were all turned away.

Due to my condition, friends and anyone other than immediate family were not allowed into my room. My doctor and parents deemed this my "time of healing." I needed peace and quiet, and I could not risk exposure to dangerous outside germs. I understood the reasons but didn't like not seeing or speaking to my friends.

Get-well cards and letters arrived en masse from friends, classmates, neighbors, and acquaintances. I still have each put away in a file folder. I look at them from time to time to remind myself how far I have come and how far I have yet to go. People to whom I had not spoken in years wrote me cards and letters expressing their well wishes.

Churches in San Francisco said masses for me.

My archbishop, high school brothers, teachers, and coaches sent me an enormous poster, with their thoughts, prayers, and best wishes written all over it.

Everyone I knew and loved reminded me that they were pulling for me.

Faith, family, true friends, and those letters kept me going in my loneliest and most dismal of hospital days. Yet, everyone was impressed with how quickly I recovered. I started my recuperation flat on my back because of all the tubes attached to me. When the tubes came out, I could sit in a chair. I was asked to sit up for eight hours a day.

Eventually, I could use a wheelchair. I would move that chair around the circle-shaped hallway within the ward with a nurse and physical therapist always by my side. When my arms were in better shape, I had better control of the wheelchair and whipped around the hospital like I ran the place.

From the wheelchair, I was upgraded to a walker. At first, it didn't seem like a promotion. I moved *fast* in my wheelchair. With the walker, I moved like a ninety-five-year-old man, shuffling slowly, one tiny step at a time. Recovery of any kind is like that, moving at a slug's speed, and ridding oneself of things that cause you hurt or harm. Deep down inside, though, I knew I was making tremendous progress.

On the day of my discharge, I was transferred to my first psychiatric ward. My emotions were haywire, from excitement to sadness, from grief to elation. I know it sounds weird, but I was excited.

In the psychiatric ward, I would trade in my walker for a cane and a back brace. What a great day that turned out to be! The bottom line is that I was so thankful to be standing and breathing.

I was so thankful to be alive.

CHAPTER 6

~

The First Hotel Stay

After the hospital, I was admitted to a psych ward in San Francisco. It would be the first of seven psychiatric wards that I would be admitted to over the next ten years. I came to call them "luxurious hotel stays."

When I arrived, I was barely moving, let alone walking.

Though I'd been treated for the injuries I'd sustained in jumping from the Golden Gate Bridge—those shattered vertebrae—I had yet to heal. Though I was happy to be alive, life had become incredibly painful.

Putting on my back brace was a nearly impossible feat I struggled with each morning. The brace was made of an extremely hard and inflexible plastic connected with industrial-grade Velcro. I hardly had the strength to move, let alone to fasten that Velcro. Velcro that was strong enough to hold me together. At least, until I could do so on my own.

Every day, I couldn't avoid my twenty-three staple, sixteen-inch scar.

With the brace, my hands would run down my side and feel the rough ripple of skin undulating between each staple scar. Flashbacks of my jump would overwhelm me. Memories of that wind, tearing me apart. That emptiness of four seconds that stretched out for far longer. The height and water closing fast. The impact of the water. Nearly drowning.

Fear set in along with regret from what I had done.

Being admitted to and living in a psych ward was, is, and never will be an easy situation.

In the wards are people who may never get out of the system, who have lived there for years. Or, others who will never reach their full potential and never become productive members of society. People stuck in the recesses of their own mind, trapped by their own thoughts. People for whom the outside world will, for as long as they live, remain as mysterious as the psych ward was to me, when I was first admitted.

And then the undeniable realization dawns on you rather soon: you are among them.

I remember other patients in that first ward cut or harmed themselves with just about anything they could get their hands on.

Once, a girl promised a nurse she would only use her plastic knife for eating. As soon as the attendant turned her back, the girl snuck from the table in the dining area clutching the little plastic knife tightly in her closed fist. She slid noiselessly through the doors into the kitchen nook where she sliced her arms open with the sideways cutting-motion you might use on meat. Her eyes were focused and determined on the spot on her arm over which the little knife scraped, attempting to create an open wound, a cut.

I happened to be there, and I attempted to grab the knife from her hand, to stop her and called for one of the nurses, yelling as loud as I could.

When they came, I was shaking more than that girl.

To her, it had just been another day in the life, as though that sort of thing was routine.

I saw people act more paranoid than I had ever been, even in my most psychotic state.

One in particular, a man I'll call Michael, would always wear the same red t-shirt and repeat aloud in a monotone voice, "They are coming for me."

The first time I met Michael, I asked, "Who?"

He immediately yelled: "The fucking FBI, the CIA, the NSA. They're all coming for me!" His voice bounced from the walls, floor and ceiling of the room we were in, muting everyone within earshot.

I never questioned him again.

Many times, I was assaulted by a few of these very troubled souls. They didn't mean to harm me, I know, but those were experiences that left me shaken, scared.

Another, "John," was locked down most days in a padded white-walled room with a soundproof door. My daily routine forced me to walk by this room. And sometimes, as I passed, I would hear him flailing around in his straightjacket bouncing from wall to wall screaming: "Where's my wife? Where's my dog? What did you do with my kids?!"

The sound of that pain was intolerable in its emptiness.

Every day when John stopped flailing from padded wall to padded wall in his straightjacket, the staff would sit down across from him and wait until his breathing became normal again. The staff member would take a breath, and say, in a voice you might hear at a funeral that his wife and kids had left him years ago. If pressed, the staff member would admit John had lost his family because of his psychosis.

The look on John's face every day as he heard that his family had abandoned him was heartbreaking.

The expression was the worst sort of loss a person could ever know.

And because John would inevitably forget this conversation and the news it carried, he will experience this loss every day for the rest of his life.

A petite woman in the ward told me over breakfast that she didn't know why they wouldn't let her have her son back. As her eyes shifted to some commotion occurring at the other end of the room, I looked at her wrists, arms, and shoulders. What once might have been smooth, slightly tan skin was now a varied landscape of mountain ranges and canyons cut with pain. From what I could see of her skin, it was riddled scars made by knives, indentations from pencils, sharp and dull, and countless other scars inflicted by unknown objects. The history of her solitude was literally inscribed on her body.

When she returned her attention back to me, I said: "They won't let you have your son back because you keep harming yourself."

She paused and nodded softly, slowly.

"I know," she said quietly. "I just can't stop."

My stomach curled, as I looked into my hands. What else was there to say?

Every time I looked at her violent and deep scar tissue, it called to mind my own scars and the scars—visible or not—that every patient in the ward carried.

The pain worsened every day.

I have always been sensitive and here, it was hard not to feel the sadness and loss from each and every person around me.

Weeks passed.

I had visitors, especially members of my family and friends who showed up in my doorway nearly every day.

I looked forward to these visits when I could laugh and talk as though nothing had changed.

I knew I was lucky for this. I savored the moments when they would come, bringing news. Stories from their own lives. Or even just a friendly smile. After all, most of the people in the hospital had no one to visit them. The staff called patients without visitors "The Forgotten." And aside from us who saw them each day—the patients and staff of the psychiatric unit—for the rest of the world, they very likely were.

During my stay at the ward, I got better. Slowly, but little by little each day was better than the one before it. As my body healed, so too did my mind.

I educated my family about my disease and I asked my doctors and psychiatrists for information about bipolar disorder. I no longer wanted to deny the reality of my condition. Instead, I wanted to learn as much as I could. I followed my treatment plan.

After a month or so, I was released. Within a few months, I felt good again.

The routine I had learned in the ward: my routine of exercise, medication, talk therapy, and social interaction *worked.*

At last. For the first time in my life, I had learned how to take steps toward my own well-being.

My family stood by my side from the day I left the ward and every day that followed. This became the catalyst of my improvement. My experiences in the hospital were powerful and gave me great hope. The days which stretched out before me appeared like happy ones.

Still, my mother was not convinced I had done the work to heal. Some days, she still isn't. She is, after all, the parent who adopted a sick child and who said I would not quit screaming for hours each night. Nothing she did would get me to stop, until, one day she said: "OK kiddo, this is it, you've got to cut this out . . . or else."

She was ready to place me back into foster care.

Sensing the finality of her words, I settled down and became calmer, more relaxed, more comfortable and serene. Her sharp words kept me with her. She is, without a doubt, a huge gift in my life. After that moment, she's never let me go.

Her skepticism of my progress shows, more than anything, she still hasn't.

Today my mother and I have a lovely relationship; we have managed to move past all of the pain caused to one another. She sees me for the man I am, she is proud of my success. Her eyes seem to sparkle when I walk into her house, the home I grew up in. Moving our relationship in the right direction has been a blessing.

I have to say, though, that I disagree with her that I am not better. The progress I made from the body that was rescued from the waters of the bay to the one that left the psychiatric ward is not the same.

But more importantly, my outlook, at last, had changed. It changed, in part, because I began to realize I could give hope to others who were struggling with mental illnesses. Day by day, I learned that following a treatment plan made the symptoms of my condition subside. The books I read on bipolar disorder helped me to understand my illness— I wished everyone with the disease would have the knowledge I'd gleaned from the books my family brought to me.

And so, when my Uncle Kevin gently mentioned that I should speak about my condition, it seemed like a natural progression for me. For as long as I can remember, helping others was my calling. But speaking to help others? Could I? I suddenly remembered attending a conference when I was a high school freshman. I walked out of the conference thinking about the public speakers that I met and heard: I could do that. I love talking and I love helping people.

Eventually, I would realize that path as my own and become a professional public speaker—and an advocate for mental health. That old conference had a lot to do with this decision. But so did one man: my Uncle Kevin.

CHAPTER 7

~

The Great One

In and out of the hospital I had the most help from one man. The one person who guided me often was my uncle Kevin. Imagine a short stocky man with broad widened shoulders over a portly frame, pasty white skin, and a very big belly and you've got a great sense of my uncle Kevin.

He's an Irish gentleman, bald with large, thick-framed eyeglasses. He never leaves the house without his tweed Kangol hat perpetually perched on his head and some piece of clothing with the Local 856 Union Logo on it somewhere. His hands are like my father's and seem to be the size of a small gorilla's.

Or, as I like to call them "oven mitt–sized hands." As a young man, my uncle Kevin went into the seminary, devoting himself to a higher calling, but before being ordained he quit for reasons unknown to me or my family.

Uncle Kevin's next gig was as a Teamster with Local 856. He handled the union agreements with all of the major hotel chains in the San Francisco Bay Area. For years he fought for the union employees at these hotels including those at San Francisco's famed Westin. He would retire with the union, but he always stayed closely connected to the work.

He feverishly followed the union's activities and was involved in decades of democratic political campaigns, meeting and campaigning for Senator Diane Fienstein, Senator Barbara Boxer, and former House Speaker Nancy Pelosi. Kevin used to tell me stories of his "hey day" at his favorite job when he was assigned to drive around the likes of Jimmy Hoffa, President Truman, and other powerful figures when they hit the city. He even ran for public office Assemblyman, against the man who would become San Francisco's Mayor, Willie Brown. In fact, I still have his running poster hanging in my garage. He was edged out of the race, though, when a local paper found him dead drunk in his automobile.

For nearly thirty years, Kevin lived his life drunk. But then, something changed. He stopped drinking. And so, during the final thirty years of his life, Kevin became a true humanitarian.

He saved countless lives across the Bay Area. He would find those living with alcoholism or they would find him, and then he'd bring them through a rigid ninety-day Alcoholics Anonymous meeting spree. He would not give up on them until they were safe and done with alcohol.

All my life, I heard about the people Kevin saved. Those near him—particularly his friends—told me he'd helped them in some life-altering way. I heard this from so many people I often wondered how far his influence reached. Nearly everyone around him would tell me, "Uncle Kevin saved my life." The big guy would reach out to those in peril, those suffering from addiction or alcoholism. I am a testament to this because Kevin Joseph Ryan had an oven mitt–sized hand in saving my life, too.

We were never close when I was a kid, which is funny in a way because I'm named after him. Yet, as a semi-grownup, we have become close. In fact, he was the most empathetic man I have ever known, while still being the toughest. After my suicide attempt, Uncle Kevin was there when I left the hospital and became a patient in the psychiatric ward. He, perhaps more than anyone else, knew exactly what I needed: to be present. And, unlike so many others that would walk away, he was there.

Day in and day out, he was there, his figure filling in the space of the hallways and the doorway to my room. He brought me books about bipolar disorder to feed my growing curiosity about my condition. He also brought me books about suicide prevention awareness and public speaking manuals. Although I never acquired a legitimate college degree, Uncle Kevin made sure I would be educated. Some of the books which have helped lay the groundwork for my life's journey included *How to Love Someone with Bipolar Disorder*, *Bipolar for Dummies*, *An Unquiet Mind*, and *Night Falls Fast*. Along with the books, he would always bring me the latest X-Men comic book and a delicious cup of the soup-of-the-day from one of his favorite places around the city to feed my body and my soul.

I can still smell those aromas of chicken noodle, minestrone, potato leek, split pea. I can taste the hot soup dancing on my tongue, warming me from the inside out. His heart of gold worried about me—to show his concern and love, he would take me to an independent film that happened to be playing that day, or he would give me a couple of twenty dollar bills to feed my weekly comic book need. No matter how worried he was about me, though, Kevin was the only one who never walked on eggshells around me. He was always upfront, brusque, direct, and sincere.

When I was well enough to leave each hospital ward I was ever in, he'd take me on road trips, both in and out of the city. One of my favorite spots was when we would go over to Cole Valley. There, he would take me to an eatery around the corner from where he lived that specialized in serving crepes. I am sure that the entire family has eaten at that restaurant with him at one point or another, along with a great deal of friends.

My appetite never matched Uncle Kevin's. Boy, could he put down a plate! And if he felt the necessity, he could clear two! No matter where we went, though, I'd always ask if I could help with the bill. You already know his answer. He waved his arm like a gangster and put a mean grimace on his face. He topped that off with his signature East Coast tone, "Are you kiddin' me?" Once, while Kevin was driving me home from a daily outing, I tried to tell him where to make the next left turn. He rarely got angry, but this time, he'd had enough of my backseat driving: "Jesus Christ, don't you think I know where the hell I'm going? I drive you here every fuckin' day don't I? What'd ya think, I'd forget?" He then gave me a tempered knuckle sandwich to the back of the head.

When I started to get teary-eyed, he said, "What the hell are you crying for?" as if the knuckle sandwich had already been forgotten.

"Are you gonna hit me again?" I asked, feeling vulnerable.

"Hit you? I would never hit you!" He said, blinking in shock behind his big, thick-rimmed glasses. He had no idea what just occurred. By this time, Uncle Kevin was seventy-six years old, and beginning to forget quite a bit. I silently nodded, sensing things were off. I couldn't ever be mad at Uncle Kevin. I understood. Hell, I laugh about it today. It's one of my favorite stories. It just goes to show you that no one's perfect. It was clear to me that malice was never intended.

I owe my career to Uncle Kevin. Although I have known for as long as I can remember that I love helping people, Uncle Kevin was instrumental in helping me to realize that public speaking was my calling.

As a four-year-old kid, I remember approaching my neighbor as he maneuvered around the lawn with his giant John Deere lawnmower and asking him—over the loud hum of the engine—whether he needed my help. When I was in third grade and the eighth graders picked on the scrawny kids, I would consistently intervene, even if there wasn't anything I could do, then. "Helping" has always been my guiding light. But Uncle Kevin showed me how to focus my good intentions even during the most dire of hospital stays. I didn't realize it at the time, but with each book he brought me, Uncle Kevin was helping me to build a future as a successful mental health advocate and public speaker.

If you want to know the truth, I originally thought that speaking publicly—telling my story—was a ridiculous idea. From the beginning of my suffering, I had no clear vision about how to find my inner voice, to say nothing of my public one. A big part of my journey was realizing that we must all find our voices eventually. And when we do, it becomes our duty to look out for those who were hurting and in pain.

Likewise, if you have a voice that you are willing to share with the public, one you think expresses great healing, maturing, and leaves thoughts in the minds of those listening to find help, you should use it if you can, if it's right for you.

Uncle Kevin believed in me. No other action demonstrated this more than his insistence that I actually read the books he gave me. He said it would give me a leg up in the work I did. Kevin felt that I would also learn a plethora of information on my own brain illness as well. With such focused and personal topics on public speaking, suicide prevention, behavioral and mental health, I learned more than I might have in a school setting with the books he gave me.

When I began to speak publicly, he would come to all of my speeches and tell me what I did wrong and exactly what I "nailed on the head." He would also say, in a loud raspy voice: "Yah did good kid!" His praise was not easily won, however. If I disappointed him, he'd tell me that, too. If I used a tool from one of the books, or a quote, I could see the elation in his eyes as he sat in the audience. Afterward, he would say, "Way to go, you got that from . . ." and then he'd name the chapter title and sometimes even the page number from the book.

That was one of the best things about Kevin: the way he would know a book inside-and-out right down to the information found on each of its pages. He always read the books he gave me first and then he would tell me where to search and what to use in my presentations. He didn't just do this for me and he didn't just do it only for those he loved. He gave these kinds of gifts to anyone and everyone he thought needed his help.

My first professional public speech happened the year following my jump off the Golden Gate Bridge. No longer nineteen years old with ideations of suicide, there I stood trying, hoping to affect change for the attentive, young bodies before me.

Beads of sweat, noticeable only to me, made their way down my neck and back.

I was very nervous. I looked down at my blue buttoned-down collared short-sleeved shirt, adjusting an invisible wrinkle. My eyes continued their path to my shaky left hand which held the first version of my virgin speech.

If I had the ability then to look into the future I would have seen a decade of public presentations, and work in the mental health and suicide prevention fields. For this moment, I was a changed man, with a purpose. My confidence, however, that this presentation would actually help anyone was low. I worried about its effect. Only time would tell.

Public speaking—and advocating mental health—is my life's work and the most intense passion I have had for anything besides my lovely wife. Years would pass and I would solidify myself as a working part of mental health activism, public speaking, and writing. Various audiences would see me fighting for Senator Patrick Kennedy's Mental Health Parity Bill, working to raise the net or rail at the Golden Gate Bridge, and helping to install a barrier on the Santa Barbara Cold Spring Canyon Bridge (the day after it went up, a woman would try to kill herself there and when she saw the barrier she called the police and was saved).

Yet on that day in 2001, I was aware of none of my future realities; on that day, I was barely even present. In front of my eyes sat 120 seventh and eighth graders. Some seemed eager to hear what I had to say, sitting forward in their seats watching me with intent eyes. They had all been told that I had an amazing story to share with them, and as young as they were it was clear by the chatter that a few of these bright shining lights were skeptical of what I was about to say.

I stood before each forest green sweater and grey slacks and plaid skirt wearing uniformed kid, and I prayed, God, please let me do a good job. I cleared my throat and the tears began to well up in my eyes.

Not now! I thought.

Though they were the first tears that would creep into my eyes before a presentation, they would not be the last. They were, in a way, inevitable. This story is so close to my heart. Every time I tell it, I experience the truth I saw not only on that long fall but all that I've been through every single day since.

The students were instructed by my former teacher at this very school, my favorite instructor from that school whom I recall with pride. "Please be silent." It was as if I were in seventh grade all over again. Even my mind quieted to her calm tone. Monsignor Gerrard was there too, he nodded at me with a smile and an encouraging blink.

I wrote the speech the night before; I stayed up until three in the morning spilling my guts out via keyboard onto the computer screen. Out of the printer that night came seventeen pages.

The story of my life.

I thought to myself, how could my life even fit on seventeen pages? How was this possible?

I woke up early that morning to practice. Again and again I read through and rearranged the speech. The running time was about forty-five minutes.

My stage time arrived.

But instead of a stage, it was more like small room with a white eraser board which would stand behind me. The audience fell silent as I took my place, mid-stage, before them.

I took a deep breath, and yet another deep breath, and then one more for good measure.

The students' legs were all crossed, they were anxious to hear my words. This brought me back to the days when I attended this school, the days when I sat in that exact manner focusing on one of my teachers.

As I looked down upon them, each of the seventh and eighth graders hung onto my every move, and every word. They were at attention. My introduction was over: "Hello. My name is Kevin Hines and I have bipolar disorder." I was terrified out of my wits; there was no turning back.

I began:

I am here to tell you my life story and in turn teach you about mental illness. I am here to teach you about the brain disease bipolar disorder, an imbalance of chemicals in one's brain that affects the way a person thinks, acts, or feels. In the year 2000, on September 25 to be exact, I attempted to take my own life by jumping off of the Golden Gate Bridge. That was the single worst day of my life, and the single greatest mistake I have ever made.

Those were the very first three sentences that came off my paper, out of my mouth, and into their ears. The students gasped after the paragraph was finished.

During my first-ever professional public talk, I shuddered, my nerves on edge, and tears streamed from my eyes at every emotional turn of the story. Some of the students cried along with me, as though feeling my pain.

I could barely finish the presentation, but I did. The feeling was overwhelming; it reminded me of getting on the wrestling mat with little experience and only a week's learned technique but with a heart that raced, anticipating an unexpected win. Losing the first match, but going on to win the next too, the crowd watching my every move. The way wrestling matches made me feel: overwhelmed and alive. That is how it felt to tell my story to others.

I had no microphone, no lapel, or sound feedback. It was just me, the students, teachers, and the Monsignor.

My voice and their thoughts.

I never had trouble with making my voice loud enough to be heard. Thank goodness for that.

It took courage for me to tell my story here like this for the first time. In a sense, I had overcome my inner and outer demons by talking about what I'd been through. Yet, when I was finally able to, that was when I realized the story's power.

The air in the room was clean, crisp and when it was inhaled a sense of strength ran through me. I felt this might very well be what it was all for. The pain, the struggle, the abundance of misery, all for this moment in my life when I would stand before a room of others and describe it all.

All of this was so that I could learn life's ultimate lesson, and then go out teaching that lesson to everyone who was willing to listen.

First I had to help myself gain clarity and then it was up to me to use the tale for good, spreading it as far and wide as I possibly could. Even though I stuttered at some points, stammered and took long tear-filled pauses, these kids were right with me, listening intently to every word breathed.

When it came time to end my presentation, few eyes were dry.

Applause roared, filling the room.

Then, the question and answer period began. One, then another, then like a wave in a high school basketball game, the hands popped up. After a question was answered, more hands rose. For such a young group, their questions were inquisitive and intelligent, evidence of how closely they listened to my story.

"What led you to the Golden Gate Bridge?"

"Why didn't you ask for help?"

"How did your parents react in the hospital?"

"How many people does this kind of mental illness affect in America?"

This last question gave me a quiet smile. For some, listening to me speak hadn't been about one person's life. It was for a greater cause—it was about saving other lives.

Two weeks later, Monsignor Gerrard called me to the Convent and into his office. He had something for me, he said.

It was a package, and I opened it there before him.

The cover art was beautiful: a picture drawn by students of Jesus, a cross behind him, all drawn in detail and vibrant colors. Inside the folded picture were exactly 120 letters, one from each of the 120 students who witnessed my first speech.

The letters expressed the students' thoughts about the talk. Some expressed gratitude for having heard my speech. Other letters—six to be exact—expressed suicidal thoughts or inclinations. Because of the courage I displayed in telling my story, these students felt safe telling me theirs. Yet, because the students were minors, every letter was screened. All of those students who had expressed suicidal ideations were counseled, all of those students were guided to help. This first presentation and its outcome have played an enormous role in my continuous work in these respective fields. Every time I think of throwing in the towel, and I admit sometimes I do, someone, somewhere across the country or the globe reaches out to me after a speech or media appearance and explains that it was my story that changed or saved a life.

I don't know about you, but I cannot walk away from that. I must soldier on. I must continue to try and help those around me.

All of those students from my first presentation are alive today. And it is because of people like them that I will forever keep working to help those in need. Yes this life is a gift, but a gift meant to be shared.

This was the first time I replayed Brother Daniel and his remarks from the hospital in my head. "When you get well, you have to talk about this." That, paired with the books Uncle Kevin gave me and his encouragement that my story should be shared.

That was the first time I owned the power of the human voice—*my* voice. That was the day I knew what I had to do, by any means necessary. I had to talk openly and honestly to anyone, any group, or any organization willing to listen. I had to reach as many people around the world as was possible.

CHAPTER 8

~

Breakdown City—
Locked Up Again

I had begun to believe that the bridge was only the beginning.

Or, more accurately, the bridge was only the first of many beginnings I would experience over the next ten years.

After my release from the hospital and during the treatment that followed, I began to believe that I was completely healed.

I would never become so "mentally ill" again. I had just given my first public speech, which was a huge success. Soon after, my father and I reached out to see if anyone wanted to hear this "amazing story of triumph over adversity," as he called it. We were semi-successful that first year in reaching a few thousand people.

Remaining mentally healthy, however, was not as easy as I thought it would be.

One year after jumping from the Golden Gate Bridge, I moved from San Francisco to San Jose to attend another university with a "special disability" admission. An old friend and counselor from my high school, now the counseling director at the university, granted the special admission. At twenty years old, I was excited to begin a new chapter in my life.

However, the excitement of this honor faded fast. Shortly after the first semester came to a close, I could not sustain my mental wellness. I worsened my case.

I started drinking again while taking the medication my doctor prescribed to me to keep the psychosis at bay. With it, my paranoia—the nagging idea that people around me were plotting against me or planning to harm me—vanished. But the medication's effects were dampened with the introduction of alcohol into my system.

I had been taking a powerful antipsychotic, a mood stabilizer, and two antidepressants. No one's medication works the same for any other individual, so I will not name them here. They were strong and, if taken accurately within a strict routine, extremely helpful. However, I was a far cry from following that routine.

The medications were in place to keep me sane, to help me function in school and in society. They could not, however, stand alone. The routine consisted of talk therapy, education as to my particular brain illness, healthy eating habits, good sleep pattern (circadian rhythm), regular cardiovascular exercise, and more. This group of regular activities had been helping me stay stable, but due to naïveté, I dropped this working scale completely.

I stopped taking my medication (thinking I no longer needed it—I was *well*) and continued drinking heavily. This made my psychosis—and, the delusions—worse. Not only was I feeling the full effects of bipolar disorder, which are challenging enough, my psychosis once again had full reign over my mental stability. Daily activities like attending classes or having a conversation with a friend became difficult, if not impossible, with the passing of each day. In fact, each day without my medication I withdrew more into myself, believing everyone around me hated me, or at the most extreme, wanted me dead.

As figures passed me in the hallways, I'd avert my eyes away from theirs. I don't remember raising my hand a single time in class after I'd stopped my meds. Instead, I sat in class, nervous nearly to the point of shaking, hardly able to wait for the hour to end when I'd rise, grab my books, and run from the lecture hall stuffed with other students whom I thought loathed my presence there.

Now, these are all signs that I recognize of my particular condition that I work each and every day to control. But then, I was young and I'd survived jumping off the Golden Gate Bridge. In my peculiar way, I reasoned: if I could survive that, I could survive anything at all. What was a touch of depression, after all? Maybe, I thought, people really *didn't* like me that much. I had *survived*. I was alive and I was going to college.

Therefore, I believed that I was cured. I was just another college student who did what (I reasoned) college students do: sleeping irregularly due to the demands of my classes and the demands of the social life I'd found there. Drinking more than anyone should.

The brief period of mental peace I'd known after the psych ward became only a memory, half forgotten in this new life that was darkened day by day.

My low point came at a sprinter's pace when I missed seven days of medication.

To put it bluntly, I'd become a complete wreck. My manic behavior was visible to all who knew me well at college. I would speak rapidly without an end in sight. I would display grandiose tendencies, like telling my friends that I would soon become dean of the university, and believing it to be true. The excessive spending of my trust fund was a problem. I had acquaintances drive me to the local mall, where I spent up to seven grand at one clothing store. I even spent a couple grand on my friends, and then a few hundred dollars on those I barely knew. The money well was about to dry up and I felt completely broken, again.

The mania led me straight up, skyrocketing my inability to gauge what was going on. Then, as is the nature of bipolar disorder, the highs lead straight to a painful and deep depression. When the depressive lows hit, I could barely muster enough energy to get out of bed. I was falling behind in every class, I lay in bed staring at the ceiling light, and when I closed my eyes all I could see was the bright glare of that light. The pain I felt was internal, but so real. Those former thoughts of uselessness returned. What was I capable of if I could not even get out of bed to go to class? I could not socialize or eat.

The ups and downs of my illness had once again taken their natural course, I had gone up, and came crashing down. I had not asked for help, or been following any kind of reputable treatment plan. I was once again lost and I knew that my brain was trying to kill me as I fought to stay on this earth. My memory of this time is not the best, although I do know I became suicidal again. Thoughts raced in, and took over.

What follows is what was gleaned from shards of memory and the recollections of family and friends. On this day at the university, I had been coming apart at the seams, friends had recollections of me spouting off at the mouth about death, and loss of those I loved most. They heard me as I recited portions of the book of Revelation in the Old Testament. I had a copy from one of the schools Bible study groups. I was reading it day and night preparing for the end of my days. Apparently, I scared quite a few friends of mine into a worried panic. Then like a magician, I disappeared. For some time my whereabouts were unknown. I had gone to my room, contemplating suicide.

Eight stories up, I sat on the windowsill of my open dorm window with the screen removed from the window pane and propped against the wall behind me. My legs dangled into the dark open air, still cold, since spring hadn't yet arrived. My hands rested on each side of me, spread on the metal sill of the window.

I swung my legs whimsically as tears pricked the corners of my eyes. I watched the movement of my legs and the space between my dangling feet and the pavement of the walks on campus, eight stories below them. It was an inevitable distance for me to fall, I thought. Less than four seconds.

Once again, I was thinking about jumping.

A crashing sound behind me tore my thoughts away from the pavement below. Aaron and "Big" Chris, his teammate, pummeled at the door of my room along with a fellow by the name of D-Roque, or "The Rock," as we called him. They instinctively knew what I was contemplating. I don't remember who grabbed me first, or who pulled me from the ledge. I just remember watching myself lifted by several strong arms off the sill and into the solidity of the room.

From there, they near-carried me to the ground floor, through the foyer and then to the courtyard, out in the open, our breath becoming clouds in the cold air.

My feet on solid ground and I hadn't fallen there.

Aaron had led the charge; he was instrumental in my mental health at college from that day forward.

He personally took me to the counselor's office for evaluation the day after he and the others found me sitting on the window ledge, legs dangling. He did what I could not: admit that I still needed help.

I was not healed. Not yet. I was instructed to sign a release that stated I would not buy a weapon. I also signed a contract that I would not attempt to take my life. This was the first of many times I would sign that type of agreement.

Days after this breakdown, while trying to hide this from my family, I came down with both the flu and bronchitis.

I missed another seven days of medication, throwing me deep into manic depression. This had been a depressive "low"—one of two extreme mood swings that can affect those with bipolar. Though there were times when my thoughts raced quickly through my mind—a manic state, such a euphoric natural brain induced high that leads to saying and doing things completely out of the scope of reality—there were also the lows when it was as though my life slowed to a halt and it was all I could do to keep going. I could not eat, sleep, or even move.

Through all of this I had to be *well* because I kept trying to convince myself I did not have this stupid illness called bipolar. I was healthy. I survived. I was better. Again and again I told myself that I was mentally well although it was blatantly obvious to everyone around me that I was anything but.

Finally admitting to myself that I still needed help, and understanding I was unwell, I went to a drugstore and finally picked up my medications, my bronchitis was being taken care of with antibiotics. I wanted to see my family. I wanted to be home.

After I just got over the flu and bronchitis, I went home to San Francisco, to see my family for spring break.

My father hugged me close when I walked through the front door of the house I lived in since 1999. I was happy, too, to be home again. All those old memories from years ago came back. The holidays together. I hadn't realized how much I had missed everyone in the months away living in San Jose.

Just days into my visit home, my father was preparing to leave that weekend for work in Los Angeles. Right before he left, we had the only fight that has ever turned physical.

That night, I was in a complete manic state and he could see it. I was pacing the halls, repeating again and again how much I needed to go and see my friends who were attending a musical performance at the high school, just like the one I played a starring role in.

My dad, however, told me that I needed to stay home that night for my own safety. In my altered state of mind, I couldn't see that he was living the part of a worried parent. All I could see was his gigantic frame looming over me, trying to control me. Like an animal, I felt threatened, then I pounced. I started screaming at him.

I screamed that he could "Go and f— himself!"

And that he could "Kiss my ass!"

Through all of that, he listened calmly.

Then, I said, "You are an angry old man! I hate you, you never loved me!"

Those were the words that got to him. He grabbed me by the lapel of my pea coat, squeezed the coat arms together with me in them and threw me up against the wall, knocking down a picture in the process. He tossed me like a rag doll onto the floor in his bedroom, picked me up, and shoved me into his bed.

"You are not going anywhere!" he said.

I will never forget the look in his eyes.

With a look of desperation, he feared for my safety and what I might do to myself in that manic state of mind.

I keeled over in severe stomach pain (this kind of neurological pain occurs with those who have brain diseases and is actually quite common). He thought I was faking. I got up and took off my coat. Beneath it, I wore the Atlas, Mexico, soccer jersey he had bought me a year or so earlier.

He cornered me between his two hallway mirrors. He bent forward facing me. I was crying and puffy-eyed. He had the ugliest look on his face, one that could rival a rabid dog ready for the jugular. "Do you want to hit me? Go ahead, hit me. Give me your best shot."

I can't confirm it, but I imagine that is exactly what his father used to say to him. I replied, "Dad, I would not hit you if you hit me once; not if you hit me ten times; not if you killed me. I would never hit you."

He backed away and I thought of the times I knew of that he and his father used to get into knockdown, drag-out fistfights. My dad had never fought back against his father, until one day, when he came home and found his father, drunk and violent. Young Pat Hines, with all his might, planted a right hook on his father's jaw. That was a mistake, as his dad was an even tougher Sunset Irish longshoreman. He didn't even budge. He turned his head slightly around and said, "Don't ever do that again."

Afterward, my dad would finally realize that it was my mania speaking and not me. I had just begun my medication regimen days before. They had not yet kicked in. That night, after convincing him I was fine, I went to the high school musical.

I didn't see much of the performance because I was coughing up blood in the bathroom. Apparently the bronchitis was not finished with me yet. My friend who had picked me up that night from my home after my dad left heard me from the audience and came to my aid.

We left the program early, went out for the night—or so we thought. We visited several different nightclubs and met up with friends, but too soon it became clear to everyone involved that I was far from OK. I rambled on about being the "King of the Universe" and wanting to run for "President of the World." I was in the midst of another severe manic episode, experiencing auditory and visual hallucinations.

Once again I was broken, and my friend took me home.

All of my closest friends came to the front door, hoping to cheer me up. They all tried desperately to talk me down from my state of paranoid delusions, hallucinations, depression, and mania.

They told jokes.

Stories from past times, together.

Nothing seemed to reach me.

When my friend Ryan (who may have felt there was too much stimulation having all of those friends in one place trying to get ahold of me) took me into the bathroom and closed the door. He was the only one who seemed to get through to me. I think it was because he was so much like my father: brash, harsh, tough, and super intelligent.

He yelled to get my attention. It did not work. He then grabbed me by each shoulder. To keep my attention he shook me, then as fast as he shook me back to a semblance of reality, he stopped the movement. "Kevin, Kevin, calm down! Look at me, listen to me. Are you listening?" I could hear my dad in his voice and see his demeanor. It was like my father was right there.

He and my father both came from families riddled with pain. They were both raised in the Sunset District of San Francisco. They were both of partial Irish descent. Ryan always got through to me. Although

Ryan and I have had our fallouts, he has been a great friend throughout my life. I listened, and to an extent, I calmed down.

My mother was at the lake. She called Libby, got on the phone with me and asked if I thought I needed to go back to the hospital.

Hearing my mother's voice brought back all our moments together. More than that, she also reminded me about the absolute need for honesty.

Without a pause, I said, "I need to go to the hospital right now."

She called my Uncle Kevin, who drove me to the psychiatric unit.

My sister, Libby, also drove to the hospital with her husband, both of them in the car behind us. Once again, I was headed toward a hospital; I had become incapable of healing without major aid.

I remember sitting next to Uncle Kevin in the admitting room.

The hospital staff asked him why I was there.

Uncle Kevin heard their question but said nothing at first. His eyes darted to the empty coffee carafe in the waiting room and then to his gigantic hands before resting on me. He cleared his throat once, then again, before pausing to say, gruffly: "Suicidal."

They asked me to confirm.

I nodded, silently.

The staff assessed me further, gave me medication and placed me in a room with a yellowish-brown wooden door, white sink, soap dispenser, silver garbage bucket, and gurney. Too soon, the reality of the people around me faded and my delusions took over my field of vision. Their voices faded, too; instead of hearing what was spoken to me, my mind created its own dialogue that flooded my ears. The following is what I heard and saw.

In my delusion, I saw a hotel, like the one I used to see in the corner of my bedroom years ago. The hotel was small, as though shrunken to the size of a doll's house or a public speaker's podium. Incredibly, inside of it were nearly 15 million occupants. They all spoke with a British accent, their words indistinguishable from one another through the chatter. I began to speak to them as I had done when I experienced this hallucination in the past.

Just as before, the British occupants acknowledged I was there and began speaking to me. Soon, as always, we were having a heated conversation.

I was focused entirely on them and them on me.

Meanwhile, my favorite uncle on my mother's side walked into the room.

Uncle George. He is the kind of fella who will walk in a room and immediately tell a joke or funny story, no matter the situation. He lights up any room.

He walked in but I did not recognize him. My mind was elsewhere, focused on speaking to a group of people who did not exist.

As Uncle George approached me, I yelled: "Who the fuck are you?"

Not missing a beat, he said: "I'm your Uncle George. Kevin, it's me, Uncle George. Do you know me? Do you know who I am?"

I shook my head, trying desperately to comprehend what was happening; trying to parse what was real from what I had hallucinated.

"No, I don't know you," I said when I searched my mind for his face, coming up blank. I paused, then asked in a meek voice: "You're my uncle?"

"Your Uncle George from Arnold, California."

Maybe it was the way he said it, the soft, honest quality of his voice. "I believe you," I said. It felt like the only right thing to say.

He asked me if I heard voices.

I nodded. "Millions of them."

I told him about the hotel in the corner.

"Kevin, they're not real, but I am. You are safe now, just try and do what the doctors ask you to. I will be right outside." He gave me a hug and said: "You're OK now. You're safe now." He then excused himself from the room.

I can only imagine the conversation he held with the nursing staff.

By now I knew my father was on a plane back from LA, traveling as fast as he could to be by my side.

My mother would soon arrive from the lake as well.

I couldn't wait to see them both, though in the back of my mind, I felt sorry for the reason that caused them to come together.

The next morning, I was admitted to a new psychiatric unit.

This would be my second psych ward admission. Or, as I affectionately and humorously call them now, my "luxurious hotel" stays. Where else do you get to sleep in a bed you don't have to make and meals you don't have to make yourself? Or, breakfast in bed, every day. Same time. Same place.

This inside joke makes me smile, even on some of the worst days.

A few days later, when I was feeling better—the hallucinatory hotel and its occupants were nowhere to be found—all of the friends who had so kindly taken care of me when I needed them the most came to visit me. So did Uncle George.

Walking in the room with his bigger-than-life persona, he took control of the conversations that had been swirling in the room by saying: "Kevin, and Kevin's friends. What we have here is young man on a scale." His voice had that lilt of an announcer you might hear on TV. The booming voice, announcing something big, something grand. "Kevin here is on a sort of meter, and that isn't any ol' silly meter. We'll go ahead and call it the fucked meter." A few of my friends' faces wore shocked expressions. Others snickered, holding back their laughter. Uncle George shifted his attention from everyone to only me, asking: "Kevin, on a scale of one to ten, where do you see yourself on the fucked meter?"

No one could hold it in any longer. All of my friends burst into laughter.

Through my tears, so did I.

"A five maybe," I said.

Never missing a beat, Uncle George said, "I think your friends would agree with me when I say you're about an eleven or twelve!"

I laughed. My friends laughed. It was a light moment at a dark time.

When all my visitors left, I met the night staff.

I remember one staff member as a tall African man wearing a Bill Cosby–like sweater, you know, direct from the *The Cosby Show*. Checkered or striped, and always multicolored.

I loved his sweaters. His personality matched them: vintage and cool.

Then there was "Blondie," a nurse with bleach-blonde dyed hair.

The other staff members, however, blur into unfocused bodies. My memories of that time cross back and forth between what actually happened and what I had been imagining.

And now, I can't tell one from the other.

My intake picture shows an overweight young man with long auburn hair, a thick goatee, wearing a black pea coat that covered a blue urban-style Southpole buttoned-down shirt. I have a funny glaze over my eyes, as if I was high on an illegal substance. I wasn't.

Instead, the only thing running through my body in excess was my level of mania—another effect of my mental illness.

My case manager met with my family and me. She was amazing, and a great mental health advocate. She, my mom, and my dad spent the day in a room vigorously arguing about the procedure of my care: what I did and didn't need and what each of them was doing wrong. She assessed me and placed me on the fast track for social security disability and supplemental security income.

This meant I would be permanently labeled as physically and mentally disabled, and always in need of ongoing psychiatric medication and treatment.

During my stay in this psych ward, I was assaulted by a patient while stopping him from committing a potential rape. My memory of this is crystal clear.

One night I could not sleep, I counted shadows on the ceiling above me, waiting for the heavy sleep to fall over me from the medication the staff had given me hours earlier.

Fortunately, as it turned out, they did not knock me out. At roughly 3 a.m., I heard a brain-rattling scream. I sat up and jumped from the bed. I ran out of my room, following the horrible noise into the hallway, and found a woman, barefoot and in a hospital gown—a patient who had a room a few doors from my own—standing there.

The patient said urgently, "Come quick, we need help!"

The staff acted as though they hadn't heard anything.

I ran with her around the corner.

A stocky, distraught man who had been admitted earlier in the day stood in the middle of the hallway. He seemed to suffer from what can only be described as post-traumatic stress disorder.

He was in the midst of attempting to unzip Nurse Blondie's pants. The scream I'd heard had come from her. The patient was forcing himself upon her while undressing himself.

Without any hesitation or thought for my own safety, I jumped on his back and pulled him off her. I yelled for him to stop.

Turning away from Nurse Blondie, he threw me to the wall with one arm. Though he was short, he was much stronger than me. The expression on his face was pure hatred.

As I stood there with my back against the wall, he pulled his arm back as though he was getting ready to hit me, full force. It must have been the adrenaline because I have never acted so fast in my life. I blocked his punch with my right forearm.

I wondered if I'd be able to successfully block the next punch which, from the way things were going, would be fast approaching.

In the meantime, the female patient who brought the situation to my attention rallied the guards and the rest of the staff. I heard their footsteps echo in the hallway before I saw them arrive, in white jackets like angels.

Together, they restrained the attacker and led him to a locked and padded room. For months afterward, however, he continually "mean mugged" me with a violent looking death stare until the last day of his stay, when he then apologized for his actions. "My head wasn't straight, sorry about earlier."

I told him it would be OK if he got the help he needed. This is a crystal-clear example of what psychosis can do to a generally good person: it can literally make an average person do things they could never imagine themselves, or even want themselves to do otherwise. Mental illness changes the brain, thus it changes *you*. Even my mother during this whole time would say to me, "Kevin, you are not the son I once knew."

I certainly had not become violent against others but I had changed, my entire personality had shifted, the mental self-destruction had caused others in my life to see me differently. It had caused some of them to lose hope for my future. The man who assaulted me in the hospital and had come close to sexually assaulting a nurse may have never plummeted down that path had he been mentally well.

While there, I also met a delightful woman. Normally outspoken, eloquent and happy, her psychosis escalated rapidly when she went off her meds. An older woman in her fifties, she was, while under treatment and medication just like any other fifty-year–old woman. She had interests outside the hospital. Family and aspirations for the future that were quite normal and grounded.

In fact, every patient was like this. When we collectively followed serious and different forms of treatment, we were productive members of the ward. If we refused or had just come into the ward, we were dangerous to ourselves and others; such is the nature of these kind of behavioral health challenges.

Each of us had what I call "Jekyll and Hyde" syndrome. Every psych patient in the world, no matter their diagnosis, has a scary alter ego. In the midst of psychosis any human being can do things that they would never think of doing in their right mind.

I met another woman who liked knitting and watching black-and-white movies. When she went off her treatment routine, she liked nothing more than to scare me with the thoughts that spun from her psychosis.

As I sat reading comic books or any of the many books Uncle Kevin brought me, she would quietly creep up behind me, offering me no hint of her presence. It seems like she would wait until the moment I was the most absorbed in whatever held my attention before she would screech: "The Dominican priests are going to rape us all!"

When she approached me from the back as she often did, I would jump out of my shoes and socks. After composing myself, I had to bite my tongue almost each and every time. I knew she was sick and that she didn't mean the things she said and did.

On occasion I would calmly say things like, "There are no priests here and no one is going to hurt you. You are safe." I would say what-ever I thought would keep her calm until the staff could arrive and quell the situation from there.

It wasn't long after my admittance that I began to feel brutal stom-ach pains.

The stabbing pain was relentless.

It felt like a tiny person was stabbing me with a dagger from the in-side of my stomach, puncturing tiny holes into the air outside. At first I tried to ignore it but the pain only worsened, causing me to keel over.

The pain was so great, the nurses called in a physician.

The diagnosis: two large ulcers were eating away at the lining of my stomach. Prevacid was prescribed, a purple and black pill to stop the damage and reverse the effects of the ulcers. Thankfully, it worked like a charm.

Soon after my ulcer medication brought the immense pain to a halt, my room was changed due to the hospital taking on new patients. My new roommate was a sixty-seven-year-old white male with stark white hair, and a pair of small rimmed bifocal eye glasses. He was an ex-Navy SEAL. He was an avid reader like my great uncle and quite the philosophic fellow, old-style and slightly faded Navy tattoos and all.

After we got to know each other, he told me that if I were in the Navy, I would have been a captain because I was a "definite leader."

I enjoyed our conversations and looked forward to talking with him every day. We talked about nearly anything: world peace, politics, and faith.

He had plenty to say. Mostly I just listened.

He struck me as wise, and I enjoyed connecting with someone who seemed as put together as he was. I never had moment with him where his sanity was in question, which made me wonder.

One day I asked the question bluntly, cutting into our conversation: "Why are you here?"

"It's a long story, so I will give you the short version," he said. Without pausing, he continued, "I tried to kill myself, no need in telling you how. I had a very bad week, that added up to a very bad couple of years. I made a mistake. It won't happen again."

He went on to tell me about his family that he lost due to his instability. Unable to understand his condition, they had simply left him behind.

Every day in the hospital, my blood pressure was taken. Every day it registered a bit high due to the terrible stress I was under. I constantly had a fever as well. Each night, the door to my room stayed slightly open allowing the nursing staff to peek in on me and determine whether I was in danger of another suicide attempt.

I was always on suicide watch.

This invariably remained the same in every ward I was in, all seven psychiatric hospitals in less than ten years.

Here, I was constantly petrified.

I was afraid of patients like the one who tried to drop a right hook on my face after I stopped him from attacking a nurse.

I was afraid of those in the hospital who would find a way to harm or cut their own extremities.

I feared what diseases they may have had, and if it would spread virally, infecting me. I feared for my well-being and my ability to heal under such commanding stress. My fears were legitimate, at least some of them.

Hospitals like this in the preliminary days were cesspools for my severe paranoia. In a way, it's only human to fear that you will be influenced by your environment. In psychiatric wards, I was constantly surrounded by psychoses that seemed stranger and more terrifying than my own. I wanted to be well, after all. Yet, all around me, I was surrounded by others who were sick.

But many of my worries and fears were unfounded and ridiculous.

I believed that once I had entered into each ward, the staff would plot my assassination. Thoughts like these made it harder to heal, or to move forward in any capacity.

As days passed and the medication began to lessen my paranoia, I could better assess my progress.

As the paranoia (a huge part of my rare and specific form of bipolar disorder) subsided and the therapy—cognitive, art, and chaplain therapy—continued, I was getting better. The staff also pushed me toward a lifestyle including exercise, healthy eating habits, and regular sleeping patterns. All those elements of my altered routine helped so much.

It wasn't a walk in the park. In fact, it was all hard work. And once again, it would not be the last time that I had to go through a relapse.

I was out of the hospital in about three and a half weeks.

I was better for a while. The next year, my speaking career would again grow: help came from all directions to get my story to the masses. Suicide prevention organizations like San Francisco Suicide Prevention, the National Suicide Prevention Lifeline, the American Foundation for Suicide Prevention, SAMHSA (Substance Abuse Mental Health Services Administration), and SAVE (Suicide Awareness Voices of Education) out of Minnesota, and mental advocacy groups like the Mental Health Association of San Francisco started reaching out to me. They all wanted me to keynote their minor and major conferences and prevention walks, along with church groups catching wind of it and wanting to book me for their congregations.

Suddenly, I was in high demand and I was working hard to accommodate all the requests that came in despite being in a mentally unstable period in my life.

My life became a roller coaster for the next two years; I was constantly in and out of hospital stays. I lost weight and gained it back. I went on and off my treatment plan. I swerved on and off the road of denial. When I was on the routine, I worked hard. When I was off, I crashed, thus totaling life as one would a brand new and shiny car.

Instead of going back to San Jose, I enrolled again at a local college. I tried to stay involved with my education. I tried to stay healthy. My attempts seemed to show wonderful growth, but then I would inevitably get tired and fall off the routine that I worked so hard to achieve.

My treatment plan never actually failed me, the truth is my disease just became harder to fight. Later, when I would meet others who suffer from bipolar disorder, I realized the path to wellness is hardly ever linear and is never easily traveled. Each day is a struggle: sometimes, you come out on top, feeling happy and vibrant. But there are other days that are much harder than they should be. I tried despite the ups and downs to remain mentally well. That is all any of those suffering so terribly with mental afflictions can do, try your best to follow suggested and reputable forms of treatment.

Most people with a form of bipolar disorder have to be prepared, no matter how hard one works in fighting it, to have symptoms. The reality is that these symptoms will always occur; there is no cure. That does not mean there is no hope. One can live, like me, well most days, and be prepared and ready for the difficult to horrendous days. One can realize and be so self-aware that no matter the symptom they can live, stay mostly well, and stay alive.

I ended the year having made it two years past my jump from the Golden Gate Bridge. With the range of symptoms I experienced, the destruction of the disease, I was completely uncertain of who or what I would become. However, my vision to stand out as an agent of change remained steady and strong. While I fought to be mentally well for myself and for my family, I also fought to help others.

CHAPTER 9

~

Big Dreams, Little Stage, and Unrelenting Psychosis

My delusions of grandeur started at a very young age.

At six years old, I believed I would become a great film actor, sit on David Letterman's couch, and laugh with him and his audience, while promoting my newest film—a film that would win some coveted award. I was talking to the bathroom mirror, but in my mind, Dave and I were having a blast. He would crack a joke, then I would add to it, totally within the realm of what silliness has gone on during his tenure at *The Late Show*.

Four years after my attempt, I tried to pursue my acting dreams while auditioning for the next college musical. I auditioned with the old love song by the amazing Nat King Cole, "When I Fall in Love." In my hunt for the part, I had enlisted a voice coach who also happened to be a neighbor. I rehearsed, privately and at home, constantly.

The director of the musical was my favorite new acting teacher. I had already taken a class with her in the city. She is a wonderful teacher and a great person who always had my back and was completely understanding of my mental illness. She was even more empathetic to me than I could be to myself.

Yet, this audition would lead me straight into my third hospitalization on the third-floor lockdown unit of the psychiatric ward. This episode was due to ridiculously grandiose thinking, extreme paranoia, mania, hallucinations, and once again, suicidal thoughts.

The grandiose thinking led to my belief that I could have achievements that were completely out of reach; bipolar disorder can often be associated with such ways of thinking. The extreme paranoia reared its ugly head in conspiracy theories against me. I believed nearly everyone I knew—my family and friends—was scheming against me.

The manic and hypomanic episodes led me to campaign for the presidency of the United States at the age of seventeen and a half. I canvassed my neighborhood searching for votes that I could count on.

After these highs, though, always came the lows. When I missed some big goal, I always felt the weight of the entire world crashing in on me. Down to the lowest low, an impact not unlike those waters of the bay that had shattered my bones two years before.

Auditory and visual hallucinations—other features of bipolar disorder—kept on coming. I saw so many disturbing things: people the size of thumbs, spiders covering the surface of every object around me in a moving field of black and brown, demons coming from the ceiling to gather my soul and leave me helpless. Above all, the most pain was caused by the depression.

Once again, because of my reluctance to keep the daily routine of taking medications, pursuing therapy, and sleeping and exercising, I relapsed mentally. I stopped taking my meds; this time for about three days.

The opening day of the show I was riding high on the energy of a manic episode.

When I got home, I went to my room. No one knew I took myself off the meds that had become essential to my well-being. However, it's fairly common for those on psychiatric drugs to feel improvement then convince themselves they can live without them. Other times, if the drugs are not working or other issues surface, sufferers assume the medications do no good and give up on them altogether. I paced in my room, staring at posters and pictures of Dwayne "The Rock" Johnson, thinking to myself once again, "Why can't I be a champion like my idol?"

I began to hear the voices beckoning me; I heard very little from them since jumping off the Golden Gate Bridge. They became so faint, in fact, that I no longer mentioned them in my therapy sessions. I believed that they, too, were part of the past.

I noticed something about each poster that I had not seen before. The Rock had a scar on his left shoulder, a pretty big one. Taking my "cue" from that observation, I ran downstairs and opened every drawer, looking for something to cut myself with. I did not want to die. I just wanted to be like my idol. I also wanted the voices to go away.

I took a steak knife and began to cut a line into my right shoulder that mirrored the image in the poster. The steak knife turned out to be too dull, so I resorted to a box cutter. Pushing the sharp metal into my skin, I felt the burning pinch only for an instant before the voices vanished. Blood droplets trickled from the wound I made.

I wished I never tried this in the first place. I am the first to admit that cutting gets you nowhere fast and can lead to serious suicidal attempts down the line. That scar now protrudes from my arm where it will stay. It serves as a reminder never to engage in self-harm again.

On my way to rehearsal, I crossed a street to get some food. I wasn't paying attention—I was distracted by the throbbing pain in my shoulder from where I'd just cut myself and the twinges of a paranoid fear that everyone I knew was plotting against me— and was promptly hit by a black Honda Civic. The right front corner of the car clipped my left leg, spinning me horizontally almost 180 degrees and up in the air with my body completely horizontal about five feet off the ground.

I landed hard on the pavement. My elbow and head struck before the rest of me did.

I watched the driver continue on, as though nothing had occurred.

From the safety of the curb, people stared at me as if to say, "Serves you right, kid, for walking in front of a car." Fortunately, other than a swollen elbow and a headache, I was OK. Had I been walking two steps ahead or in more of a hurry, it would have been a different story.

I returned to the theater. I wrapped an ace bandage over and around the self-inflicted shoulder wound, going over lines in my head.

This was the night my dad and his friends were coming to see the show. This was also the night of my third psychotic breakdown, in the latter half of the second act.

It happened much like my second psychotic breakdown, the one in high school. My dad would later blame it on my dreams of acting and how they clouded my sense of reality. Maybe there is some truth in that.

Nevertheless, during the show's intermission, tears streamed from my eyes as I screamed to no one in particular: "He's judging me! He's in the audience judging me! He hates me. He doesn't want me to be his son!"

The entire cast feared that I might be on recreational drugs. They feared for my security. They feared for their own.

We got through the two-and-half-hour show and *Joseph and the Amazing Technicolor Dream Coat* opening night came to a close. That night, I had two roles in the musical. I was in nearly every scene as either an Ishmaelite or a Roman. They were two minor but important roles. For my role as an Ishmaelite, I wore a sack tied by a tethered brown rope. Later in the show, as the Roman guard, I barely wore anything.

I strode out onto the stage bare-chested and armed with a prop sword and shield, the self-inflicted wound on my shoulder glaring under the spotlight. During the rehearsals, I always dressed as a demure Roman: my costume, while fitting with the historic era, had never displayed a profuse amount of skin. This contrasted sharply with my bare chest and wounded shoulder that no one had noticed until I walked under the spotlight on the stage.

The other cast and crewmates must have thought I was crazy. They had no explanation for my decision to wear hardly anything onstage or any warning of what happened when I stepped behind the curtain.

After I exited the stage, the director took great care of me. At my request, she did not allow my father into the dressing room at first. From his seat in the audience, he would have seen my shoulder. He had figured out the cutting incident. He knew that I had become completely unstable.

Eventually, she let Dad into the dressing room. I was a wreck. When he approached me, I flinched as if he was going to hit me. Instead, he put his hand on my good shoulder and told me he loved me and that I needed to get help.

We drove to the house, grabbed shoes, a pair of pants, and a clean shirt. He also dressed the wound on my shoulder, changing my haphazard bandage for a proper one. Then, we sped to the hospital.

I would be back in the psych ward, back in pain, back in a ditch. Yet, I promised myself that this time would be different, this time I would get my act together. This time I would find hope.

CHAPTER 10

~

Lock Down—
Third Time's a Charm

I do not remember my anger the night before, and I certainly do not remember waking up in a violent rage on the day after my arrival. Yet, that was how I began my third psychiatric hospital stay in less than four years. As it turned out, I spent one month and twenty-five days in the hospital, from May 1 to June 25, 2004. This would become the longest of any of my psychiatric hospital stays. It would also prove to be the hardest.

According to reports, when I woke up that second morning, my first full day at the ward, I flipped over my wood-framed bed that weighed probably more than 200 pounds while screaming, "I hate you! I will kill you! You are the enemy!"

After the bed clattered to a standstill, I pounded my fists repeatedly into the solid walls of my room until they were scraped and bloodied. The orderlies, nurses, and security guards came to the door and politely asked me to stop. I apparently said something to the effect of, "Why don't you come in and make me!"

They obliged my request, however misguided, and entered—three guards, an orderly, and two nurses.

To say the very least, there was a struggle.

Under the power of all six of them, I went down. Many powerful milligrams of Haldol—or its proper name, Haloperidol (an antipsychotic/

tranquilizing medication)—were then shot into my rear to calm and, ultimately, to sedate me. I struggled to stay awake but surrendered to the heavy dosage, weighing me down and slipping me into another kind of darkness.

My first psychiatrist, Dr. Gregory, was originally from New York. Greg, as I called him, is an accomplished doctor in mental health, suicide prevention, and psychiatry. He started one of the more recent movements for the Golden Gate Bridge by implementing a task force to raise the rail, making it more difficult for people to jump. The raised rail would be titled the PFNC, or Psychiatric Foundation of Northern California, an organization I would lead as director. An older gentleman, Greg remains in tremendous shape thanks to a daily routine of Pilates and rigorous exercise. Though pragmatic and forthcoming, Greg is a fast talker, and if you are not paying attention, you will quite easily be lost in conversations with him. He would become a great friend. Our relationship progressed from doctor-patient, to friends, to co-authors, and then colleagues.

He said I needed a "permanent" change in my attitude to get and stay well. I would have to work, but not before I had some serious therapy. During my stay at the hospital, I moved throughout the ward engaging in art therapy, cognitive behavioral therapy, group therapy, meditation, creative writing therapy, and so many other forms of reputable therapy treatments. I did it all. I did so much therapy that by the second month I was fed up with therapies altogether. I needed a break.

By this point, my dad and I needed a serious intervention and some family therapy of our own. He'd always been critical of me when I was growing up—after all, he wanted me to the best I could be. But when he became critical about my ability to remain mentally well—about taking my medications, attending various therapies (or critical of the therapies' usefulness)—it became difficult to take. I guess I always knew he had my best interests at heart, but my mental wellness was a sore subject for me. I felt like I was doing all I could to stay well and when my dad said otherwise, I got upset.

For example, I might be having a great day at the hospital, I would have taken my meds and have a smile on my face, and then he would show up and, without meaning to, wreak havoc on my days in the ward. To me, he berated me for my lack of willingness to get well. Or, he'd demean any progress I had achieved as "not enough." No matter what I said or did, he always left angry which, in turn, made me feel as though I had failed. One day, I told the nurses, "No more Dad."

He would not be welcome in the psych unit because he was not conducive to my mental healing. The staff even placed a sign on the visitors' area window right next to the elevator leading into the ward, stating he was not allowed into the ward. In retrospect, I am sure that broke his heart. Yet, at the time I was afraid of his criticism and its ability to derail the progress I had made. In some ways, I am still intimidated by his tendency to become so angry so quickly.

My decision proved terribly embarrassing to Dad. For that, I am sorry, but I had to make the break if I was going to get back on track.

Until this relapse, some of my closest friends and my family especially had grown weary of my breakdowns. They all thought that I hadn't focused enough on my mental wellness. They didn't want to worry, constantly, that I was always on the verge of taking my own life.

Even though I was generally surrounded by those I loved, and even though they all cared deeply for me and my well-being, it didn't matter, because I sincerely felt alone as though there was not a single person who understood me. Even as my brother or sister or my mom or dad came to visit, I nonetheless felt disconnected from them. They had spent so much time worrying about me and my mental state, I understood when some stopped seeing me. They felt I needed to recuperate on my own, that I "needed time" to heal. When I saw other patients' entire families wait in that tiny holding area, being let in two at a time, I was not only jealous but quite saddened that my family did not do the same. I remember one Filipino American family who seemed to arrive in droves to see their loved one. That family never missed a day visiting their patient, not once. They came and stayed as a group, while my family would come in sprinkles here and there. Their idea was to give me the space I needed.

Although at the time it hurt, I must say, knowing that they were all so affected by this my third hospitalization, I ended up working ten times harder to find and attain a balance of good mental health. I guess their tactics worked after all.

When I was feeling isolated with my mental illness, my joke-telling and boisterous Uncle George would often come to see me. Until one day when he didn't come with jokes. He wore a serious expression on his face when he walked into my room and said it was time to have a *mano y mano*. A serious talk for a serious time.

He didn't yell. He didn't judge me or my mistakes. He came to bring me into the light. He came to save me from myself. He sat down next to me in the empty dining area and made me understand something: without family, and the will to fight adversity, what do we have?

Uncle George reached me in a way no other person at that time could. He laid it all out in the open. In so many words he told me that I was messing up big time. He let me know that my family and friends feared me staying in that ward for all of eternity, or cycling through hospitalizations until old age. He said it was all up to me, that unless I took full responsibility for my actions and inactions, I would never heal. He was the first to state that my wellness was entirely up to me.

"Kevin, me, your mom, your dad, we can fight for you until we are blue in the face, but unless you get off your ass and start fighting on your own, you will be in here or a place like this for the rest of your life!" he said.

What he said opened my eyes. When he walked back in to the waiting area and onto the elevator, my epiphany began. The very moment Uncle George left the room after our *mano y mano* talk, I said to myself, "Enough is enough. It's time."

I realized how true Uncle George's words were, I began to believe that without faith in my own ability to survive and even thrive, I would be lost indefinitely. I took a good hard look at what I had, not what I didn't. I rebuilt the strong faith in God that my family and I always had. I can only speak for myself when I say that without family, true faith, and great friends, I would not have made it past that hospital stay, nor would I be alive today.

Without my family, friends, and my faith, I certainly would not be happy now. No matter what depression, bipolar disorder, or devastating moments occur in our lives, my inner happiness will hold. I will always find hope, a future, and the epic beauty in life. The light I now carry within overshadows the dark.

My faith is the cornerstone of my life. I am not saying that faith in God or a higher power is the answer. I am saying that if you at least have some faith in yourself, it could someday save your life or the life of a loved one. That faith will also light up your potential and your path on this planet will be revealed. That faith will put you in the position to gain the newly found confidence to accomplish anything remotely and evidently plausible.

With the tools I have learned from the books Uncle Kevin brought me and the tools that Uncle George reminded me I had within, I fought hard to stay on path with my treatment and after a few weeks, I felt healed for the first time from my disease. "Healed" is a strong word, not to be confused with "cured." There is no *cure* for mental illness. But *healing* is different; with healing, the wounds have fallen to the wayside and the pain those wounds caused has subsided. It means that your future seems bright once again. It means that hope is your biggest ally. Hope gives me the joy that recovery and happiness were once again totally possible, even plausible.

I knew that I was sure to have another breakdown eventually, that this bliss could not last forever, and that another slip, relapse, or depression would be inevitable. With a mental illness, this is always a possibility that must be faced and accepted. The nature of my condition hasn't changed. Rather, it's the knowledge that I will heal again. No matter how dismal life seems, I know without a doubt that I will heal and know happiness again. This epiphany has allowed me to become more matter-of-fact about my condition, and to have more empathy toward myself—especially the battles I face each day.

Now, I can forgive myself. This new awareness also allows me to empathize with others and the struggles they face as well.

My immediate family understands more about my illness than ever before. Of course, not everyone else understands it like they do or even tries to. Sadly, due to my psychosis, I have lost close friends and family. It's been years since I've seen them on holidays or heard their voices on the telephone. Yet, I hold no ill will toward them. This sometimes happens even when mental illness is present.

Mental illness can be too much for some to bear, even if they're not the ones suffering. But I have come to understand why this is so, why some friends and family can't be near me, can't call, can't write or communicate. Maybe it would be this way anyway; maybe people just grow apart, but I have decided, that for me, no matter the reason, it's OK. I accept it. I understand. I even empathize. A mental illness can be scary if you know absolutely nothing about it. But the majority of those close to me have found a way to heal from their pain with me. If anything like this ever happened again, I am aware that all of the healing could disappear as though it never occurred.

Since my jump, my family has found some peace. Concurrently they carry the anticipation of the possibility of a relapse. I'm sure my mother and father still fear the worst—my eventual death by suicide. Pushing through that deep-seated fear is the hardest part for them.

After Uncle George came to see me, I made the decision to live mostly mentally well for the rest of my life. This was, after all, my third hospitalization, my third visit to a psych ward. The third time I might have ended my own life. In the hospital, I wrote and drew in a special hardbound journal that I still have today. I would write or draw in it every day while in the psychiatric unit. I would write poetry, short stories, and draw pictures—anything creative to express whatever I was feeling at the moment.

One day, not long after Uncle George came to visit me, I wrote a story about my attempt to climb a mountain. For me, the story was clear metaphor for exactly what I and every person with mental illness was going through. Mountain climbing was a perfect description of just how hard living with these brain illnesses can be and how hard it was to be mentally well. How sometimes I failed. But mostly, the story was about how I kept on going.

I read this every day to remind myself how important it was that I become well. It wasn't just for me—my health was something I also wanted to give to my family, those incredible people who remained by my side and who had not forgotten me.

Every day, I'd read this short story that reminded me that wellness and a bright future was just around the corner. Here is what I wrote in my journal and read to myself each day:

Short Story Written in Psychiatric Ward Journal: So I am walking up this trail . . . I am walking up, around crevices, corners and in and out of tunnels. Tunnels made by mother earth. So yeah, I am walking up this trail, always up, and never down. Well now that's not exactly true. Sometimes I go down, way down! Sometimes I think I am right back at the bottom where I began. But just when I think I end up where it all started, I see a sign that says "Almost at peak." So I know I am going in

the right direction. I keep walking. I keep on trucking. I want to get to
the top of this mountain, to achieve "total bliss." At least that's what
the long-haired, bearded man told me at the beginning of the trail.
Way, way down there. So I look down and I see where I made my first
step. Damn, I sure have walked a long way! And my asthma's not even
bothering me. I just "Keep on Keeping on." As they say.

Then I hit this huge boulder, I walk right into it, and I tell myself I
have to pay more attention. I mean this thing is huge, it's Ginormous!
Heck I can't climb it; I sure as heck can't go around it. If I do I know I'll
fall. "I know I will fail. Wait a minute!" Wait just one damn second, my
mother always said "Never Quit!" My father told me to "Erase the word
'can't' out of your dictionary!" So I stop and gather my thoughts for a
moment. "I GOT IT!" I take some pebbles from the trail, the gorgeous
green earth I'm trekking on. I take the pebbles and make a sort of powder
in my hands, you know, like a gymnast would do at the Olympics before
the biggest vault of his or her career!

I aim to take this gigantic boulder standing steadfast in my way on
like a savage beast! You better believe that I am going to obtain Total
Bliss! I have too. I then hurl my body upward to the first divot in the
boulder, then the second one, and then the third. I am half way up this
overbearing pain in my side. This alpha boulder thinks it's got the best of
me, well it's dead wrong! And I am going to reach the peak if it kills me.

"Oh, no!" I missed the divot with my foot; I am falling, back into the
pebbles, back down to the ground, hard and fast! My only chance is to
reach out and hope, no scratch that, pray that I live. Pray that I catch
myself with all of my might, and grab onto the boulder.

Well, I guess God was listening. I caught myself, and now I am dangling
from one arm on the rock. I've got one arm holding tight to one divot.
Here we go again. I hear this voice in my head, it's my mother "pick yourself up, dust yourself off, and start all over again." My mom used to recite it
again and again. As a matter of fact she used to sing it constantly. It drove
me bananas. But in my time of need I remembered it, didn't I?

And I know if I make it out of this situation alive, I'll teach it to my
kids!

At the moment I am holding on with one hand, but I remember
where the other divots are and I grab onto them with each limb. If you
could see me now, I look like your friendly neighborhood Spider-Man!
Now after sweat, blood, and tears, I somehow manage to reach the top of
this monstrosity of a boulder! I did it I am at the top, I am the man, I did
it. . . ." What the Hell?!!" This is not the top. It ain't even near the top.

The fact is that I have come this far, why stop now, why lay down. My dad did not raise a quitter. I must keep going. "Keep on Keeping on." I have got to reach eternal bliss. Whatever that means. Wait, what if the dude at the bottom was lying through his bearded face? What if his line about total bliss was total bull^%$*? Then what have I been doing on this trail for over an hour and a half!

Going back down would be plain stupid, just plain insane, and not an option.

I am getting to the top if it kills me, and it just might. My hands are bleeding and blistered, my feet are in the same shape. Man I am getting so tired and thirsty. My mind is wandering. I have got to pay attention. "Dammit, Kevin! Pay attention!"

I am so damn tired, actually dehydrated is more like it. God, I really need something to drink, some water would be nice, and yeah water would be just fine. Why in heavens name would I not bring any water? That S.O.B. down at the beginning of the trail said nothing about needing water! He did not say anything about how long this trek would be. Wait a minute, I have got to stop blaming people for my problems, and it was my fault and mine alone for neglecting to bring water. I keep on keeping on. So I keep on climbing I keep on trekking, like a champ!

I am going to the top, wait a second, what's that, it looks like drops of water coming from that cave. I am definitely gonna check that out. Wow, it's like a river in here, a very long river filled cave. Thank you, God! So I drink, I drink, I drink, and then I drink some more. I drink until I won't drink, no scratch that, until I can't drink anymore. I am completely full. But I am not at the top, not yet anyway. I will get there, that I promise you.

But first I have got to sit down, I feel like I am gonna pass out. Oh man I am dead tired. I sit down in the water filled cave to take a short break. My eyes are fighting to stay open.

"Beep, Beep, Beep." My watch just went off, my God, I slept for an hour. I slept in this cave for an hour, but you know what I have got more energy than ever. There must have been something in the water, minerals or something. Yeah, it's been decided, there were some kind of minerals in the water. So I get out of the cave and I begin to climb again. I climb, climb and I climb some more! "Do I get to the top? Do I? Do I?

You bet I do!

The Question is, "Would you?" Oh by the way, that Total Bliss thing, "That Part is completely up to you!"

And then came my big break: my third psych ward stay and an epiphany. After I decided to fight with every fiber of my being to be well, I lived mentally well for five consecutive years, between late 2004 until late 2009.

Five long and happy years. Five years in which my dad was my publicist and my guardian. He recognized the power of my story and wanted me to share it with larger audiences. Whereas he never wanted me to pursue drama—thinking I tended to forget myself in the roles I played—he latched onto my career as a public speaker and advocate for mental health. This wasn't a role—I was simply myself, speaking about my life. I was exactly who I'd been my whole life: and, by telling my story, I was saving lives.

Our proudest father-son moments then occurred: We visited a museum where my dad read about a soldier who, though afflicted by bipolar disorder, created a successful plan to lead his troops to safety. Despite his mental illness, that particular soldier had saved many lives.

My father spoke about that soldier the following night when we addressed a group of ten thousand U.S. Marines at Quantico. The noise of thousands of crisp military voices clapped up against us, louder than any applause we'd heard at that point. The experience was as invigorating as it was intimidating.

At the end of our presentation, a three-star general approached us and shook my father's hand. Then, the general gestured to me as he bellowed: "This young man is a gift from God!" All the officers replied with a powerful "Hoorah!"

Then, the general turned away from my father and reached out to shake my hand. As his hand neared mine, all I could think of was "You better have a firm handshake Hines, no fish handshake, he's a United States Marine General!" When his hand met mine, something hard and metallic was in it.

I opened my hand and looked at what he placed there. A three-starred Commanding General's Medal. I felt the weight of it in my palm, so much heavier than a quarter or any other medal or coin I ever held.

It was like the boss just gave me a promotion but one thousand times better.

The general, in some kind of bellowing whisper (if that's even possible), said, "I only give out one hundred of these in my entire military career. Don't lose it."

My father and I still talk about that day.

Those five years, from 2004 to 2009, were filled with true mental wellness. I no longer had even a trace of depression, mania, hallucinations, paranoia, or panic attacks. Through my dedication, extremely hard work with my treatment plan, my symptoms seemed to disappear. I followed my treatment plan strictly, I still took my medications, and I ate healthfully, had a regular sleep pattern, and exercised each and every day. I read up on my type of bipolar disorder and wrote a contract to myself, identifying what I had to do to stay well. I had scheduled each day with certain tasks like waking up and running every morning at 6 a.m., my meals were sectioned out at the same time every day. I took my meds daily at the same times as well. Everything became pure routine. This is actually how most people find and attain wellness most days with a mild to severe mental disorder. This kind of routine is the key.

What a joy, though, to feel mentally *well*. I was free from myself, free from my pain, free and filled with hope. I'll never forget those five years.

I'll always hold onto them, for it is those moments I think of when I fall into depression today, or when I have a "bad mental health hour, day, month or year."

I was happy for thousands of days.

I can still have that wellness, if I only keep on climbing.

CHAPTER 11

~

The Epiphany and the Gift

I could not keep looping in and out of psychosis for the rest of my life. I had seen things in psychiatric wards no person should ever have to see. I gained an unending respect for the nurses and doctors who treated me at those hospitals and psych wards. During that third hospital stay at the "luxurious hotel," with a great deal of help I pulled myself out of depression and suicidal ideation. I regained my mental health and have managed to stay out of psychiatric wards for five years.

When I participated more in my treatment and made the commitment, the goal became evident, the picture became clear. I was destined for a greater existence, a better life. I was destined to exist in a life lived well, at least the majority of the time.

My family and friends deserved to live without fear of my imminent demise by suicide, and they deserved to see the day when I would no longer end up in places like these.

A month into my hospital stay, I found myself waiting for a bed in a home for those with mental illnesses. I grew antsy as the days grew longer. I wanted the wishing to end and the fun to begin.

I asked an interim case manager if I could volunteer for the hospital while still a patient. This was unprecedented and probably prohibited. My original case manager would have said "No," but she was off for the week.

My case manager was a firecracker, an amazing lady with a fierceness and determination to get her patients well and fast. I respected her a great deal. In fact, she and George held a great powwow during my stay. Since she was on vacation, though, I tried to take over the place. I filed paperwork, organized closets of clothing from patients who had already been discharged from the hospital while taking some of that clothing for myself (with permission from hospital staff who assured me the original owners would not be returning for it).

While everyone else was wearing hospital gear, a terrible teal-hued shapeless hospital gown with matching hospital pants, I walked around the hospital in a Ralph Lauren double-breasted university label polo suit—just because I could. I always had a clipboard in hand. I looked official. Admittedly, though, the clipboard had mostly doodles on it.

My favorite task was making the morning, afternoon, and evening announcements. Sometimes to the chagrin of the staff, I did them with an enthusiasm rarely given to the topics addressed in those announcements: menu items at the upcoming meal, or reminders of upcoming events that might interfere with the ward's usual routine.

When I recited the announcements, they would go something like this:

"All right everyone, the time has come, breakfast is here, now have some fun, come one come all either do or do not, for your breakfast is here, get it while it's hot!"

One day, a young man rolled in on a gurney.

He had been taking drugs.

He was almost lifeless.

Catatonic, they called him.

He didn't move much and could not talk. Within weeks, he would eventually stand and walk, but his movements were labored and slow.

My first one-on-one encounter with him scared me to death.

While I exercised, pumping my arms and legs to the beat of the music, the catatonic patient lurched to my "exercise room" and placed his entire face on the small box glass window on the door. As sweat trickled down my cheek, I happened to look toward the door and saw his wan face perched there, staring at me.

I nearly jumped out of my skin.

He just stood there, wide-eyed.

Not knowing quite else what to do—it was awkward exercising while he watched me with that indescribable look on his face—I opened the door and asked: "Do you want to join me?"

There was no response.

I tried another question: "Would you like to sit down?"

As if in response, he walked in slowly, and sat. He didn't move a muscle, not even the ones in his eyes. He simply stared ahead of him, blankly, for an hour while I did my aerobics.

After that day, I made it a point to talk to him daily for the next week and a half.

If you ever get to know me, you will realize that I can talk.

And not just talk, but *talk*.

Talk about *anything*.

Any*thing* under the sun for more than seconds or minutes.

I can talk for hours. Days, if need be.

Let's put it this way: I bet I could win a talking ultra-marathon, talking sunup to sundown and still be talking.

I talked with him day-in and day-out.

If you want to know the truth, I wanted him to utter one sentence and come out of his semicatatonic state. I wanted to know about his life. How he came to the hospital. Like so many others I met, I wanted to hear his story.

But day-in and day-out he was always silent. Even after hours of me talking, pausing after a question I'd asked. He would always answer with that blank stare, offering nothing.

One by one, I met his family when they visited. I watched them, and later, talked to them, hoping to glean clues about his life. To know more about this silent set of eyes that watched me each day. That blinked in response to my questions. But who never said a word.

His family came in massive groups, filling the hallways with the sounds of their shoes squeaking on the floor and the murmur of their conversations a constant, echoing hum. Only two at a time were allowed to see him during visiting hours. The rest stayed in the visitors' box, patiently waiting their turns.

One day, as I rambled on about nothing, he turned to me and looked at me with widened eyes, filled with an expression I hadn't seen before.

That was a first, I thought.

I stopped talking. Something had changed. I studied his expression. Then, I knew: he *really* looked into my eyes.

Just as I was about to say something else, he cocked his head in my direction and said haltingly, "Jesus Christ man, you talk too much! Man, I know you're whole life's story! For crying out loud, give me a break!"

Clipboard in hand, I had just finished making the afternoon announcements. I was wearing my Ralph Lauren salmon-colored polo shirt and khaki shorts with sandals (from the giveaway closet). Even with the sandals, I was a step above the hospital staff in terms of fashion. If anyone looked *official*, it was me.

A woman tapped me on my left shoulder.

I turned around. She was the most beautiful woman I had ever seen.

"Do you work here?" she asked.

I looked at her and then at the nurses. The looks on their faces framed the question which must have been rolling in their minds: *What is he gonna say?*

One of the nurses even smirked at me and waited with bated breath for my response.

A huge smile crossed my face. "I'm a volunteer," I said, which was technically true. I waited for her to contradict me, but the woman didn't.

"Maybe you can help me. I'm looking for my cousin."

She told me his name. The kid who had been in a semi catatonic state.

Nodding as officially as I could, I said: "Right this way, miss."

My only mistake of the day was letting him see me as I guided her to his door, only five down from my own. I stepped to the side of his room, praying he would not rat me out. I heard her say: "Your nursing staff is so nice."

He stood outside his door, looked right at me and said, "Who, that guy? That guy's crazy. He jumped off the Golden Gate Bridge! Stay away from that guy!"

She let out a big gulp and said: "Oh my God, he could have killed me!"

Obviously, she'd never been in a place like this before.

Eventually, though, he and I became great friends. I spent time with the entire family. As for his beautiful cousin and me, we fell in love and began dating several months after my release from the hospital. We were married approximately two years later at our neighborhood parish church.

Uncle Kevin was the first person I told about proposing to the wonderful woman who would become my wife. I called him that day and blurted the news before he had time to say much else other than "hello." I could hear him tearing up on the phone. His voice even cracked a bit.

Then he said, "I love you, Kevin. I'm taking you two to breakfast, tomorrow morning, Louie's at nine. Don't be late!"

Uncle Kevin gave us a celebration fit for a king and queen. I devoured a large stack of pancakes and bacon. Later, regarding the marriage, he pulled me aside, away from the table and told me in no uncertain terms, "You better not fuck this up!"

I don't understand how my wife does it. There are so many times that I am irritable and moody. I swing up and crash down. Hard. Both ways. I go left and I sway right. After all, I still have bipolar disorder.

Despite all of that, she married me, knowing full well what and whom she was marrying.

Her mother warned her before our wedding. She said, "You're going to have a very difficult life if you marry him."

Even though I'm a staunch mental health advocate, public speaker, and activist, I know, from my life, that I will break from time to time. Her mom was deathly afraid for her daughter's well-being.

How could she not be?

I learned so much from my many stays in psychiatric wards. Families left fathers, brothers, sisters, and wives in those places. They left them to forget them.

It was easier, in other words, to live without them than to live with them. But my wife remains by my side despite the awful lows that occasionally occur.

My wife is an angel. Scratch that—she is a saint. The sheer imbalance of my psyche could throw off a Mack truck barreling down the road at 200 miles per hour.

Yet, I work each day to stay mentally well. I take my meds as prescribed daily on a timely basis. I also have a daily exercise routine and

I eat healthy foods most days, even though I love a tasty Taco Bell nacho platter.

But only once in awhile.

I practice deep breathing drills when I have panic attacks to calm me. I wake up and go to bed at the same time nearly every day as much as possible. This routine helps keep me balanced.

However, none of that stops my symptoms from occurring or taking over in unsuspecting moments. Like the saying goes, "I don't know how she does it. But boy, am I glad that she does."

I am so happy that she is willing and able to put up with such a relentless battle. I sincerely appreciate every second of our time together. Of course, it destroys her to see me taken away and locked up in a facility for weeks or sometimes months on end.

That has happened four times since we met. Since we married.

No matter the stress, my wife recognizes that sometimes she must do what is necessary. Even when she doesn't want to because it means letting me go back into the same hospital ward—or one similar where she found me.

Yet, knowing that's what heals me is completely necessary. In the years that have passed I've found there is nothing I could do through the destruction of my illness that could push her away to the point of no return. She fights the battles with me.

She suffers with me.

Spouses, parents, siblings, and children with a family member who is afflicted with a mental illness suffer, too. Some of you may be sitting next to, or living every day with such people right now. Understanding that the ones closest to you need to know you appreciate all they do to help you maintain your mental health is key.

Yet, often, those individuals, whom you love and who love you go underappreciated. They are tormented by the pain we feel without a hint of gratitude.

The people closest to those with a diagnosed or undiagnosed mental strife suffer just about as much as we do. Our actions affect all those around us, and it's time to recognize and thank the ones who stand by our side.

Those personal protectors.

To all of those, including my wife, I have one thing to say: Thank you, from the bottom of my heart.

CHAPTER 12

~

Five Years of Happiness

I gained admission to a halfway home for those with mental and behavioral health challenges who had exited inpatient psychiatric care
and were on the mend. This halfway house was part of a community
of "houses" in San Francisco that provides housing and counseling for
vulnerable adults living with serious mental illnesses and has been in
existence for more than sixty-five years. They have helped save more
lives than most San Francisco organizations could have done in such
a relatively short period. To live there, you must demonstrate that you
have a feasible plan for moving forward. You can't live there forever, after all. You need to know how to manage yourself and how, sooner than
you think, you'll pay rent and manage the outside world in addition to
managing the mental illness that landed you there in the first place.

I entered the home, a gigantic sixteen-room Victorian building,
painted a muted yellow—like the San Francisco sun in spring—with a
white trim around the windows, steps and balconies. A tall, flowering
tree stood outside the front steps, offering pink blossoms in spring. I
remember them, especially, those early moments I stepped outside to
run or walk, or even to breathe the air, happy to be alive. I had been
in a psychiatric ward for months. This was my first time "outside."
My Ralph Lauren blazers now meant nothing. The first time without

morning, afternoon, or evening announcements, where I could be predictably silly.

Here, nothing was predictable. Although I wanted to be on my own—to live my own life again—facing that reality was scary. There were so many times I wanted to quit and return to the psych ward where I always knew my exact place and schedule. Yet, after two months in the psych ward, I knew I had to move forward with my life. Granted, it wasn't easy. As a matter of fact, it was a hell of an endurance test—but let me tell you, it was worth it.

I moved everything I owned into the fourth floor bedroom, room sixteen. The room was small and square with a window that looked out onto Jackson—the street for which this particular house was named. There were two twin beds, one on each side of the cramped room under each windowsill. In fact, the room had nearly two of everything: two dressers, two desks. But just one tiny closet. And the entire house would have to share a bathroom.

I moved in with a young black man who was in and out of jail, and he was intimidating. He was a physically large young man with a dark, pain-filled past.

Among other drugs he had been addicted to cocaine. He might have been in rehab when I became his roommate but I can't be sure. When I think of him today, the first emotion to surface is fear. My first night, I had a terrible nightmare that he brutally attacked me while I slept. The nightmare was so real that I woke up in a cold sweat to find him sleeping soundly in the bed across the room from me, barely lit save for the light from a distant streetlamp that streamed through our window.

During our time at the Jackson house together, my roommate and I clashed on a regular basis. On one occasion, we had a heated argument and he backhanded me in the face, causing my cheek to swell and bruise. I do not remember what was said but the argument started because I sat in his favorite living room seat.

Even though he was quickly reprimanded, his action only strengthened and solidified my terror of him.

When I first entered the halfway house, I was still in the process of healing mentally from the psych ward. I even had a serious mix-up with my insurance and the pharmacy, which lead me to a very quick and miserable psychotic episode. On the day of my arrival, I was given a prescription to pick up my medications at a nearby pharmacy. I had to get used to the area and even though the house has a thirty-day proba-tionary period, the housemates were allowed to pick up meds, purchase food outside of the home, and other similar tasks. We were not permit-ted to go out at night, use illegal drugs or alcohol, or stay overnight at a friend's home. Those would get us expelled from the house in those first thirty days.

I entered the nearest pharmacy, assuming that my meds would be ready for pick up. When I entered the pharmacy I waited my turn in line to pick up my medications from the counter. By the time I arrived at the head of the line and stated my name, I heard something unex-pected from the attendant: "Mr. Hines, your insurance does not cover these medications."

My jaw literally dropped and my eyes watered with near-tears. I worked so hard to obtain a form of wellness. I struggled, fought, and prayed. This day did not seem to be for me. I envisioned my life without my treatment: all that I worked so hard for falling off of a monstrous cliff back into great depression, psychosis, and I heard the footsteps of fear grasping at my soul.

I did the only thing I could: I argued with the lady. I said: "I will die without these medications, I could die, please is there anything you can do to help me, I need my meds." She swiftly replied without feeling that: "You need to take it up with your insurance carrier."

The worst part was that this should have been handled by the hospital prior to my release so I would not have to face this issue. Not knowing what else to say or do, I walked out of the drugstore, looked up the hill and began to tear up. Tears slowly slide down my heartbroken cheek. The system had failed me once more.

When I got to that corner, standing by a trashcan was a homeless man. He looked up at me, smiled, and said "It could be worse." When I arrived at the halfway home, I went into the main office across from the stairs and explained my plight to the counselor available. They could do nothing for me at the moment. My only recourse would be to go to an Emergency Psychiatric Services Center first thing the following morning, and they would give me bus tokens to do so.

Weighed down with fear, sadness, and hate for the pharmacy and this situation, I somberly walked step by step up my new home's stairway. Floor by floor I cried more heavily. I got to my room and called my Uncle George. He assured me that it was just a hiccup and I had to keep it together and get to that service center in the morning. He even asked me if I wanted him to come and "straighten these people out." I told him I could handle it on my own.

That night I slept for less than three hours because the fear, worry, and pain had rushed in where confidence and inner calm had once been. My biggest fear was that full psychosis and rehospitalization was once again right around the corner if I did not get my meds soon and keep on routine. I lay awake in my unfamiliar bed staring at the ceiling most of the night, something I was not unaccustomed to since the development of my disease. I prayed all night that the next day things would be resolved.

Lying awake, 6:00 a.m. quickly approached and I wasted no time in getting ready to go to the Emergency Psychiatric Services Center. I had gone to bed in the clothes worn the night before: a Roca Wear basketball outfit, looking like a mockup of a Harlem Globetrotters game shorts and tank top. I also put on my white, neon orange, and aqua-rimed Timberlands (which I still use today), took my house key and walked out the front door.

The service center was on Turk Street, in a dangerous neighborhood of San Francisco. It was near a block which had many gang-to-gang and gang-to-police shootouts. I trembled at the thought and got on one bus then walked the rest of the way. I arrived at the address the attendant at the halfway house had written down for me the day before. A line formed in front of the center's closed doors. The center opened at 8 a.m., and the time was only 6:45 a.m. I was not the first in line.

I could restrain my worry, paranoia, and fear no longer. I sat on the curb in front of the center, frantically writing illegible poetry into my journal. It was clear I was rapid "cycling" (something that occurs with my type of bipolar disorder and can happen even after a good mentally healthy run). I wrote in the same journal that I kept in the psychiatric unit. Within its burgundy velvet cover, all of my darkest days of the ward stay were cataloged inside. Tears flowed down my face. I was having a full psychotic episode. Not to be confused with a relapse of suicidal thought, this episode had been just recently triggered and this episode was situational. I dropped the journal curbside and broke down completely, losing control of my mental state. Along with the cascade of tears, mucous dripped from my nose as I sobbed, catching mouthfuls of air. I wiped my running nose with my red, white, and blue Roca Wear tank.

As I cried, a tall, gray-haired, black gentleman stood behind me, muttering things I could not understand. The man had a bag of what looked like seeds in his left hand. He put his right hand firmly on my shoulder, as if to say I was going to be OK. Then, he swiftly spread the seeds all around my sides and back, as fast as he did that, a flurry of pigeons flapped all around me. A couple birds landed on my shoulder, resting for a moment. For whatever reason, this created a rush of pins and needles throughout my body, then calm, even a soothing feeling from deep within me. The man behind me must have known he'd have this kind of effect.

As the birds' wings fluttered around me, the man continued his incomprehensible muttering. Even though I couldn't understand what he was saying, I fully understood his actions. There is no other way to describe this moment; it was as if the man was angelic, like he was sent to me, to raise me up, making me understand that no matter what I had gone through, where I had been, or what lay ahead, it would be OK. No matter what, I would survive, I would live well, I would eventually thrive.

After that feeling of peace came over me, I got back in line, with a newfound resolve. Eight a.m. approached. Around 9 a.m., I entered the building, not knowing what to expect. Would they help me, would I get medication to tide me over for a few days while I figured out this insurance debacle? Even though I hoped this would be the end of this episode, sadly the answer would be *no*. After speaking with numerous attendants, the center's main doctor spoke to me—they all told me there was nothing they could do. Even so, I was determined.

I left the building and slowly I walked back to the halfway house, trying to think of other ways to solve this problem. When I arrived, the staff members asked if my problem was fixed. I shook my head—unlike the day before, however, the staff members became as determined as

I was to help me live mentally well. Over the next few days and with the help of the staff, the hassle was set right and I finally obtained my much-needed medications.

Over the next thirty days of my probationary period, the halfway house therapists and counselors conducted a full assessment of my stability. During that time, I also broke several house rules. The most severe rule I broke was sneaking out to party at night. I never drank while out on the town with my friends, but we always went to a few bars.

One night while out with one of my oldest friends, Brent, I nearly got into a lot of trouble. After leaving a bar on Union Street in San Francisco with a very drunk Brent, we crossed Fillmore and Union Streets and while we did, a young, agitated, and inebriated black man started walking in our direction, yelling: "Waz up whiteys, why you wearing that fit it ain't for you!"

His attention was directed at me. That night, I had on a velour jumpsuit, and a do-rag (one of many I owned), and he assumed that I was white and determined that I should not be wearing such garb.

While steadying Brent, I confronted him, "Why do you care what I wear, you don't know me." He got closer and he was clearly itching for a fight. I was on probation and already breaking the rules by being out at night. I walked up to a solid parking meter, I pushed up my sleeves, looked directly into his eyes, and said "You see this? This is your face." I reached back with all my strength and right-hooked the meter as hard as I could. My hand never retracted, I kept it on the meter once I hit it. The reverberation slid through my fist to my forearm, and then I felt it in my shoulder. Thankfully he turned on his heel and walked away. I released my fist, my adrenaline was so high that I did not immediately feel the pain, or the subsequent injury until much later.

The next morning, I took myself to a doctor's clinic to have my hand X-rayed. I obliterated the third knuckle on my right hand. The knuckle shattered to dust and I felt like a complete moron for what I did the night before. Worse than that, the doctors could do nothing for me. The knuckle had to heal on its own, form scar tissue around it, and I had to deal with the pain every day.

Meanwhile, the thirty days were passing by at the speed of a large slug. I was bored silly and every weekend I would find some way to get out at night. One weekend in particular, I told the front desk that I was headed to my mother's for the next two days. Instead I went with Brent to the Russian River. My mom had no idea that I had used her as my "patsy." After I was gone for a day, the house grew suspicious and called her. She let them know I had not been with her at all. When I returned I was given the third degree and was on probation from my probation. I was lucky I wasn't kicked out.

Yet, the house gave me a second chance (I seem to get a lot of those). Soon after, I stepped in line. I was back on the right meds and treatment plan. Once again, I recalled my epiphany that I could live mentally well, and the promise I made to my family, my faith, and myself. Overnight, I woke up with a new mind-set. My health was up to me! I had to follow a direct path to wellness.

One morning soon after my epiphany, I awoke at 5 a.m. I put on my running gear and stepped out into the cool, foggy San Francisco morning. I ran from Jackson and Fillmore streets down to the Marina. From there, I continued down to the end of Crissy Field, back to Fillmore and the Marina, and then up the hill and home. I started doing this every day, the run became like second nature to me. The distance I covered was irrelevant. The endorphins were what I craved.

Every day since I arrived at the house, I went straight to the gym on the third floor. It was small, and with little equipment, but just enough of what was needed. In between the running and working out in the small gym, I lost more than fifty pounds in just over three months. It was not just a habit—I became addicted to exercise. And little by little—almost without my noticing, I became happier and more mentally well.

Thanks to my treatment at the halfway house, thanks to the people who ran the house, and thanks to my motivation to be mentally well, I stayed healthy for the next five years without any major episodes of mania, paranoia, depression, or even one hospitalization.

Every weekday, a patient in the house had the opportunity to cook for the other twenty-two housemates. Always a big task, but definitely fun, was juggling pots of boiling water for pasta and chopping vegetables for salads.

And then, the meal: all of us seated at one table to taste.

Believe me, mental health patients will let you know when your cooking *sucks*. Thankfully, that only happened to me twice. For the first three times that my cooking day came up, I made chicken soft tacos with all the fixings. The first two times I was praised for my amazing tacos, but by the third installment of Kev's Tacos, people wanted change.

"Kevin, we are sick of Taco Tuesdays!" (My cooking days always seemed to fall on Tuesdays.)

Or my personal favorite: "Do you know how to cook anything but *tacos?!*"

So for my fourth highly anticipated cook day, I attempted something like never before, chicken lasagna. I was taking a risk, and I was filled with nerves. I found a recipe and help from the one resident who was 100 percent Italian. Basically she was my sous chef—or I was hers. Either way, the lasagna was a hit and for the next three Tuesdays that I cooked I made that same dish and interestingly enough, no one ever seemed to get tired of that.

My next try at the table I made meatloaf. It was a flop and, boy, did I hear about it.

My time at the halfway house was about to come to an end. I was in my room shadow boxing or, as I saw it, fighting with my inner demons. It was a cramped room, and I took one step too far forward. My left fist went straight through the dry wall.

"Oh, shit!" I yelled.

I paced the room, wondering how I would handle telling this to my head counselor. I knew this action might get me out of the house. I tried to explain to the powers that be that it was simply an accident. But in their minds I was already given a second, and even a third, chance. Despite my explanation, I was told I was no longer wanted by some at the home, and that the time had come for me to move on to more permanent housing. I was appreciative to them for not putting me immediately out on the street. They even arranged for an interview with another home for those with behavioral health challenges. I did very well in the interview and ended up staying at this new place for almost eight months.

While at this house I enrolled once again at college and started looking for a job. I took a few courses: some art classes, an African American history course, and English 101. In the late afternoons I worked at a 24-Hour Fitness Kids Club, where I would be in charge of twenty-three children, ages twelve months to twelve years old. On slow days, the job was a cake walk. But on those inevitable days when every parent who worked out at the club all converged their workouts upon one day, it was a *nightmare*. Everyone who worked there might have experienced something like mania on days like those. Yet, most days I loved my job and I was good at interacting with the kids. I had great relationships with clients and coworkers; I could not have asked for things to be much better. That was near the end of 2004 and the next two years would prove to be a couple of my favorites.

One day, while working at 24-Hour Fitness, I received a call from a man named Scott, the former principal of a high school for the arts in San Francisco, and the current principal of a similar school in Oakland. Scott had my name from two years earlier, when I was looking for places to present my story. I went to the school when my younger brother attended it, walked up to Scott and gave him my first business card. One I made on my old iMac. I remember the cards clearly. They were awkward and disproportionately cut. Yet, they were my first business cards that designated me as a public speaker.

He remembered the card, pulled it out one day. Apparently I never changed the phone number.

Scott offered me an interview for the position as the recruitment coordinator and activities director of the school. While I answered questions in my interview, my father sat by my side. He wanted to make sure they were aware of my mental illness, and that there had to be some special circumstances for me to take the job. Scott called me soon after our interview and said "The job is yours if you want it."

Without a pause, I told him, "Yes," and I held the position for the two-year granted time, all of 2005 and all of 2006. It wasn't easy: the school was made aware of my mental health, but I was to perform all the functions the position required of me.

Life kept getting better and better. I was physically fit for the first time in years, since my jump from the Golden Gate Bridge. I followed my treatment plan and I was the happiest I'd been in a good long while. When I left the second halfway home, I was looking forward to my new job, my new *life*. College classes were going well, too. I couldn't wait to start living this new life I'd hardly imagined for myself only months before.

As recruitment coordinator and activities director of the school, I broke up fights and got screamed at by hoodlums. Of the many more "expected" tasks I did, I remember admitting students to the Wellness Center. One in particular, a freshman boy, had written a suicide note that day that I found among his things. With the help of other staff members, we led him to the Wellness Center, preventing the suicide he'd planned. During all of this great work, I kept speaking publicly; I was with a particular speakers bureau that was founded by Tipper Gore during a White House Mental Health Campaign. With the bureau I traveled all over the country speaking to youth and helping them talk openly about mental illness and suicide prevention. I honed my speaking skills and reached a large audience.

This was also the time I grew closer and closer to my then-girlfriend and soon-to-be wife. I loved her from the moment I laid eyes on her. We had been dating since October 2004—nearly two years. We were madly in love and I could not wait to ask her to marry me, but I needed some time to plan it right. I asked her to marry me at 12:15 a.m. on our dating anniversary in October 2006, and we were wed the following June. The wedding was big, epic. It was and still is the best day of my life!

All of this time, between the first hospitalization and now, I had been speaking in public about mental wellness. I spoke about preventing suicide and finding hope through the "Black Dog" of depression.

Even when I was at my worst struggling to find my own way back to health, I would help others with my words.

In 2006, another aspect of my life was about to change. When I was an activities coordinator at the high school, I was constantly around families. Moms and dads, sisters and brothers. I thought more about my own biological family once again. Where were they? For as long as I could remember, one wish has been more important to me than any other my entire life: to know my biological family.

I have always wanted to meet them.

I've wanted this even when I thought I hated my birth parents for "leaving me."

I wanted to know them, to wrap my arms around my mother, my brother, and my father, all at once. I always imagined what it would be like to have Christmas with them or Easter. What type of tree would we have? Would my biological father have encouraged my love for superheroes like Pat and Debi Hines had?

I was always curious about what they looked like in person. What their skin felt like—clammy or soft or rough or smooth, delicate. Just like mine. What the sounds of their voices were like—sharp or quiet. If they liked to talk as much as I do.

And out of all this questioning, each and every day since my jump, I constantly wonder if I had any biological relatives in the country outside the father, mother, and brother I had already lost.

Although I knew relatively little about my biological family, I had already been told that either one or both of my parents had manic depression; today it's called bipolar disorder, the brain disease I live with.

Yet, I could not believe the paperwork I read which claimed I was English, Irish, and Italian. While nothing is wrong with that particular mix of ethnicities, it just wasn't *all* of me. Somehow I knew my heritage was much more complicated than that. I could feel it beneath my skin.

I also knew this from the few pictures I saw of my birth mom and dad. My father looked Mexican more than anything else, with dark eyes and hair and a smattering of dark freckles across the bridge of his nose.

In the photos I have seen, my biological mom, Angela, looked very exotic and beautiful.

"So, you're American," is what people said when I would tell them about my biological parents and their imagined ethnicities.

In some ways, I guess they're right. I'm as complicated as nearly everybody is these days. Yet, I take pride in every aspect of my heritage.

Seven years after I jumped from the Golden Gate Bridge, I reached out to a friend on the San Francisco Mental Health Board, the executive director, with the goal of finally finding the remaining members of my biological family.

I handed her all the information I knew: a small stack of documents I managed to accumulate in recent months. My friend said she was glad to help in any way she could. She warned me beforehand, though, "You might not find anything at all."

After a warning like that, I didn't expect her search to turn up much more than I already had, on my own. However, the opposite happened.

She discovered that my father was half-Mexican and half-Italian. She found that my mother was a curious blend of Jamaican, Sephardic Jew, English, Scottish, Arawak Indian, Portuguese, Irish, and African. And, after a lifetime of not knowing, it's nice to finally have some idea of where I am from. When I told Patrick and Debi of my true ethnicity, their replies were simple, it did not matter to them what I was, it only mattered to them how healthy or well I worked to be.

My friend uncovered my birth mother's last known address.

She also found out that just a few years before I began looking, Marcia had passed away due to a drug overdose.

Then, she surprised me.

After handing me a scrap of paper with a number scrawled across it, my friend smiled widely, saying: "Kevin, I've got great news. I've found your biological sister."

I called the number immediately and left a lengthy message.

"Hello," I said reading the name beneath the phone number. Saying her name for the first time was strange and beautiful. A sister I'd never known.

I continued, "My name is Kevin Hines. It used to be Giovanni Gabriel Prasad Ferraris. I think I am your brother and that you're my sister. Please call me, my number is. . . ."

But she did not call me back immediately. Every time my phone rang, my heart jumped in expectation only to be let down by voices I already knew, and who already knew me. She didn't call that day. She didn't call that week. Or even that year.

I was devastated. I worried that the only link to my past had disappeared—vanished—before I even had a chance to explore it. My career as a public speaker would bring my biological family back to me.

In 2009 I was nominated for—and won—a coveted Paramount Studios Hollywood/Government (Substance Abuse Mental Health Administration) issued "Voice Award" for my work in both the suicide prevention and mental health fields. When I gave my acceptance speech, I stood onstage next to rapper-turned-actor/activist Ice-T and acclaimed actor Richard Dreyfus.

The audience gasped when they heard that I survived the jump off the Golden Gate Bridge. They only heard stories about suicide attempts off San Francisco's famed bridge and those stories did not end with a man onstage speaking, speaking, and living.

In 2009 I would also hear the voice of my biological sister. Two years after I'd reached out to her and had no response she saw me on the ABC newsmagazine show *20/20* with John Stossel. He had been interviewing me about surviving the jump from the Golden Gate Bridge. She was in her bathroom fixing her hair while a friend watched the show. She heard my name along with what I had done for suicide prevention. She ran out of the bathroom, looked at my image on the screen, and said "I think that's my brother."

She hadn't returned my call because, at the time, she had been taking care of our mother and carrying out arrangements after her passing. With the loss of her mother, she wasn't prepared to see or meet me—she was still dealing with the loss of a family member. Yet, she took my serendipitous appearance on this show as a sign. She recognized the name from my phone message and decided it must have been fate when she happened to watch my story on TV.

This time, she called me.

Before she could finish her sentence, I said, "My sister?"

"Yes."

"So, I'm really your brother?" I asked.

That was one of the best days of my life. We met at a coffee shop in the city. She looked just like our mother did in the photographs I'd seen. That day, she wore a red sundress giving her skin the same glow I saw captured on film a lifetime ago. Of my biological mother.

Through her, I met our brother, whom I had no idea existed. He was equally as cool and bore a striking resemblance to me. He's a handsome dude, a surfer, cyclist, and practically a rock star, with shaggy long black curly hair. Both are (technically) my half siblings. We all shared the same mother, but they had a different father than I did. Neither of them have a diagnosed mental illness. Both of them are amazing, beautiful people.

Shortly after our reuniting, I would also meet aunts, uncles, and cousins, some of whom lived on the East Coast. My search for family—and heritage—was finally complete.

My adoptive family could not have been more accepting and understanding. They always knew of my desire to meet and be a part of my biological families' lives. They were great in the aspect that both my mother and father each held separate dinners to meet and get to know my biological siblings. Nothing's ever perfect—not everyone sees eye to eye on everything—but we are all one family now.

Just as my newly found sister and I were getting to know each other, I slipped. I found out what I wanted to know for my whole life, and yet, it wasn't enough. Nothing, perhaps, ever will be. Life isn't that simple for me.

Out of what seemed like nowhere, my antipsychotic medication stopped working as it sometimes will because of the particular challenges presented by my type of bipolar disorder.

It was as though I stopped taking them all, which I hadn't.

What stopped was my mental wellness. It was 2009 and I had five years without a single psychotic break. I recognized the symptoms; I feared them. And they were back, once again. My wife and I were still in the coveted honeymoon stage where each day seemed new and exciting.

I had every reason to be happy. My marriage was great. I knew my biological family. I followed my treatment plan to the letter but I was once again experiencing symptoms of my mental illness.

Paranoia and psychosis crept in, taking little pieces of happiness at first. And then, grabbing entire moments, then days and then everything I treasured in my life.

I was lying on the couch in our apartment. I was tired from a hard day's work. I stared at the ceiling, trying to relax, trying to close my eyes. I couldn't, though. I felt as though someone was watching me. "They" were coming to get us. "They" were going to take all this away from my wife and me. These were common thoughts for me.

Yet, instead of some unnamed menace, this time, I thought it was someone I knew. An imaginary friend who would come and kill me and my wife.

I sat up.

The hairs on my arms and legs stood straight into the quiet air of our apartment. I strained to hear the footsteps I knew were there: evidence that there was someone here to kill me.

I thought I heard them through the noise of my own breath. I wanted to hurt the assailant. Moving quickly from the couch to the closet in the hall, I grabbed a hammer in one hand and golf club in the other. I heard something at the door.

Got you, I thought. I got ready, held both the hammer and the club high, ready to knock the eyeballs out of whomever was behind that door.

My wife gasped as she opened the door, a brown paper sack of groceries in one hand, coming home from her workday. Her brown eyes—eyes I knew and loved and cherished—blinked back tears at me, clotting her lashes together. God, I should have known her, letting go of the hammer and club.

But I didn't.

"Who are you, what do you want?" I asked, my eyes bulging, my arms ready to strike.

She blinked a few times before answering. "It's me, your wife. I love you, put down the club and hammer." She moved toward me, one hand outstretched, a peace offering. "Let's sit down and talk."

I yelled, "You won't take me! You can't take me!"

Tears released from her eyes.

That episode nearly broke her.

On June 17, 2009, nine years after my jump, I asked to be taken to the psychiatric hospital where I would surrender myself to the care of the staff as well as the personal care of my long-time clinician and friend, Dr. Gregory.

CHAPTER 13

~

Moving in Reverse

While writing this book in 2009, I had a psychotic episode. It would be my fourth since the year 2000 when I jumped from the Golden Gate Bridge. At first, the hospital stay was brutal—they always are. Just as with my prior hospitalizations, the last few months before this episode I had become increasingly paranoid, depressed, and yes, suicidal. I know that I would not do my book any justice if I left this crucially important part out.

I did everything in my power before the fourth hospitalization to stay mentally well, but something occurred that was more powerful than my best efforts: my antipsychotic medication once again stopped working.

I was on a slow but obvious downward spiral for months.

After all of my healing. After the five long and prosperous years I enjoyed without one hospitalization, life went south. I literally did everything in my power, up to that point, to stay mentally healthy. I pushed myself to the limits to stay above water and of keen mind.

Yet, nothing worked.

My routine of a healthy diet, regular cardiovascular exercise, timed meals, continued education about my disease, biweekly cognitive behavioral therapy, and a regular sleeping pattern could not help me when my antipsychotic medication "pooped out."

"Pooped out."

This is the term often used when a medication is taken for a number of years and begins to fizzle out, eventually ceasing to work entirely. The diminishing effect of this particular medication led me down another slippery slope of those familiar paranoid delusions that mark my type of bipolar disorder.

I thought everyone was out to get me. And then, as unbelievable as it sounds, I was convinced my wife and father were going to kill me. Thoughts swam through my head about the various ways they would do this. And that was how I knew my medications were not working like they should and that it was time, once again, for me to seek professional help.

One morning, I prepared myself to attend therapy. I woke, drank coffee, and showered.

My wife, whom I believed would stab me at any moment, was drying her hair after her shower. When the hum from the hairdryer stopped, I asked her reflection, standing behind her and looking at us both in the mirror: "Are you going to kill me?"

I asked this question a lot in recent weeks, so she was ready for it.

She replied, thoughtfully, to my ridiculous question: "No, Kevin, that will never happen. As a matter of fact, I will be the first person to protect you always. So will your dad. We would never hurt you, we love you."

Tears began to stream down my face.

I looked at my wife and said, "Can you promise me that? Can you give me your word?"

My actions and words were so unlike me. Everything about me that morning told her I was no longer quite myself.

Yet, she kept her composure. Her eyes said so much in those moments of silence between us and the question I knew was coming.

She asked, "Kevin, do you need to go to the hospital?"

I nodded but paused before I said anything, knowing what she was asking without saying it. Finally, I said, "I might, but I am going to therapy first, maybe it will help alleviate my rapid, psychotic thoughts."

She nodded, "OK."

Most people in my situation, or one like it, are not as self-aware as I had become through a decade of dealing with this internal and arduous battle. I learned the signs of my medication pooping out and I learned simple things to calm myself down. I also learned the importance of finding myself outside help if I thought about suicide again. But still, I was not myself and my wife could see that.

Yet, knowing me as she does, my wife stayed calm. She later told me that she thought to herself, "If he even thinks about killing himself, he'll tell me or his family."

I felt the same way. I still feel the same way. That's a promise I made myself while the cold San Francisco Bay water swirled around me and a sea lion held me up. And of all the times I've found myself in a hospital and family members come, acting like that sea lion. They all hold me up. And when they aren't there, I have to do it myself. I'll always say when I need to go, even when I don't want to.

I will never die by suicide.

I promised my wife that no matter how painful it was to hear the truth, I would tell her. I promised God, my family, and friends a long time ago that, no matter what I endured mentally, and no matter what lay in my path, I would not die by suicide.

I intend to keep that promise forever.

My wife dropped me off at therapy as she did the morning before. She told me she loved me, and continued off to work downtown in San Francisco's financial district.

While entering the clinic where I received my mental health care, I realized that if I did not gather myself together soon, I would end up back in the hospital. I attended this clinic for more than five years. The outside of the clinic was simple and kept its patients' anonymity intact. Inside the mirrored double doors a waiting room contained surprisingly comfortable plastic chairs with metal legs. The floors were gray and carpeted, and to the immediate right of the doors was a coffee and tea stand where one of the social security–receiving patients sold beverages.

I went to the secretary's window and requested my therapist by name. Without much of a wait, my therapist led me to her office. The session went well, although a depression loomed over me. When this happens I begin to feel as though I am useless, and not worthy of the love of others. This is huge commonality between those who suffer from depression or bipolar disorder. My therapist asked me if I was suicidal, and at that moment I had no thoughts of harming myself, so I said "No." However, the worst was just around the corner.

When I finished therapy, I called my wife and told her that I felt like a complete burden. I was angry—not with her, but with me. A horrible thought entered my mind, as if not that of my own conscious. I abruptly said, "I should just go back to the bridge and this time, get the job done!"

My wife asked me to promise that I would wait patiently by the clinic and go nowhere—she would ask her mother to pick me up right away.

I promised that I would not move from the exact spot where I was standing. Reluctantly.

My wife's mom and brother were on their way. They reached me in fifteen or twenty minutes. I talked aloud to myself the entire time I waited, shadow boxing with myself, fighting the demons in my mind, tears welling up in my eyes. I told the evil part of me, the one who has never stopped reminding me that I need to die, "Shut up! I won't do it!"

Then, I saw the K-line bus approaching in the direction that would take me back to the bridge. It was the bus line I took nine years before. The evil voice on my right shoulder screamed in my head, *"Take it. You're worthless."* Then it whispered, *"You have to die, you cannot escape me."*

Yet, I held my position as the bus passed. I turned toward the clinic. I let out a big sigh. The voice in my head whispered, *"Pussy!"* I kept walking in the same direction. Toward the clinic. Toward life.

My mother-in-law and brother-in-law pulled up next to me. I jumped in the car, buckled my seat belt, and watched the sidewalk become urban-blur.

I broke into tears that slid furiously down my face. I told my mother-in-law and brother-in-law that I did not want to die, but I thought I had to.

I heard my father's calm words in my head: "Kevin, this too shall pass. It always does."

As I sat in the backseat of the car, safety-belted in place, my wife called me. My brother-in-law, turned around and said, as I had the phone pressed to my ear, "We're almost there, Kev; hang tight."

At that moment, I told that dastardly demon on my right shoulder to shut up! They took me to my home. They inquired as to whether I would be OK home by myself.

"Yes," I said.

I apologized to my in-laws and walked up the stairs to the front door of my home.

I opened and closed it; letting the silence settle for a moment. The stillness. The solidity of my life.

Then, I called my wife to let her know that I was safe.

When I heard her voice, the feeling and suicidal thoughts subsided.

For the first time in several months, I felt peace.

It only lasted a few minutes.

Shortly after I was dropped off, my wife arrived. She left work early to make sure I was OK. She asked about all of my suicidal thoughts and said I must tell my clinical team at the O.M.I. Family Therapy Clinic the very next day that I was suicidal and psychotic once again.

I agreed without another word. My emotions were exhausted. So was my body. We went to bed early. Before we slept, my wife and I, as we do every night, prayed that this entire episode would leave my body and exit my mind.

I hoped that this time, it would.

The next morning before dawn, I woke up, looked in the bathroom mirror and was immediately filled with extreme paranoia, depression, and wildly racing negative thoughts.

I waited for my wife to wake. And per our usual, we made coffee and ate breakfast together.

I said nothing about my mental state.

My wife dropped me off at the cafe across from therapy at 9:00 a.m.

The cafe was the same one that I had been frequenting for the last ten years, since my high school days. As far as cafes go, it's not the fanciest, with a bar where you order coffee and a cushioned bench to the left where three round tables sit with iron-rod chairs opposite. Outside are tables, too, in the atrium whose "ceiling" opens to the San Francisco sky.

It was the same place from which my brother-in-law and mother-in-law picked me up from the day before. I know everyone there. And they know me: Kevin, the regular. Kevin, who drinks a quadruple shot vanilla latte.

They knew me, though, as Kevin, a "normal" guy.

This day, though, that would change. That day they would witness another version of Kevin—the Kevin who has bipolar disorder with psychotic features. They would see me speaking to myself, casting nervous glances to everyone in the cafe as though I was suspicious of them. They would see me write furiously in my journal, tears sliding down my face as though I was in complete misery.

My father gave me a pocket-sized notebook that morning. Concerned about my recent descent into psychosis yet again, he stopped by my apartment before going to his office.

The notebook was about as large as the palm of my hand. As he handed it to me, he said he wanted me to use it to record all of my paranoid, depressive thoughts.

He wanted me to get those thoughts out of my head and onto paper. Once on paper, he thought, I would release them from my mind, ultimately forgetting they ever existed.

After ordering a banana and a bottle of water, I sat down at my favorite round, four-person table, took out the notebook, and began writing down my thoughts.

Frantically.

My hand could hardly keep up with them: every thought, paranoid delusion, and whatever else came to me in the moment flowed out of my mind and into this pocket-sized journal.

CHAPTER 14

~

Chronicles of Redemption and a Modicum of Success

Here is what I wrote in my new pocket sized journal and what I remembered that day in my favorite cafe fueled by an unripe banana and a bottle of water:

. . . Chronicles of My Psychotic Mind . . .
She [my wife] will kill me, eventually
Or, they will kill me, Or, Dad will kill me,
A sniper will kill me; Buildings will come alive & kill me
A car will burst into flames, explode, and kill me
"THEY ARE COMING!" [A constant thought in my head.]
Or, "They are here"
"Constant feelings that I have to die by my own hands,
"Call my wife" I think the "They" is actually "ME"
I feel like a total burden,
Like I don't deserve to exist
My family hates me but pretend to love me
Same about my wife's family
My wife & Dad are plotting to kill me sometime in the next few
    months....
I know none of this is the "Real Reality"
But only my "Distorted Reality"
In the last 4–6 months thoughts of suicide have increased not decreased

> Zoloft not working, still depressed most days
> Wake up in mild psychosis
> Feel like I'm going to die very soon
> Probably before I'm 30 years old, 2 years to go
> So confused, trying to hold it together externally
> Bad movie need help
> If it doesn't get better might have to go to the Hospital soon
> Don't want that, don't want Hospital
> I feel like I'm stuck in a fucking recurring nightmare.
> When people look in my direction they are trying to kill me,
> or they are talking bad about me.
> My father loves me He would not kill me, why would he want me dead
> I'm so tired of all this emotional/mental stress
> "SUICIDE IS NOT THE ANSWER" "PERMANENT SOLUTION
> TO A TEMPORARY PROBLEM" "I WILL NOT DIE BY SUICIDE
> EVER"
> Why is this happening to me, most likely pills not working?

On this same day, after writing in my journal, I remembered the one time my dad and I almost physically fought. I was in a manic state and couldn't understand why he wouldn't let me leave the house and hang out with my friends.

"You never loved me!" I screamed at him.

I know I broke his heart that day.

Still, he held onto me. He cared. "You aren't going anywhere!" he said, firm and steady. I will never forget the look in his eyes. Desperation, yes. But another emotion I hadn't realized then, but that I realized now, in memory.

Love.

Even though all I wanted to do was leave, he held onto me.

I remember my mother's doubts that I was well after my first stay in a psych ward following my jump from the Golden Gate Bridge. In so many ways, she had been right to worry. In fact, my entire life, I've exhausted my mom with my constant sicknesses.

I don't know how she hasn't given up.

When I was very young, she nearly took me back to social services, even though she wanted to keep me. "I've been your staunchest supporter, but you are making me crazy! You have got to settle in!" she had said to infant me. She would tell me this story later as a way of saying we were meant to be mother and son. I would also read this story in her old journal, the one she kept about the process, difficulty, and joy of adopting me. It's funny, I sometimes wonder if this was an early indication of the challenges I would face with bipolar disorder.

I screamed and clung to her. I had what the doctors called "bowel irritability secondary to emotional trauma." This was only the beginning of my issues with the world, of challenges I have to face and overcome.

I looked up from my pocket journal, momentarily released from my thoughts. I glanced around the cafe to see if anyone had been spying on me while I was surrounded by my words, my thoughts. A couple sitting at the table next to be was chatting. A man read the paper, sipping coffee, three tables away from me. The baristas filled orders for the people standing in line. Out of all those people in the cafe, not a single one was looking in my direction.

I realized I needed serious help, but my therapy session was thirty minutes away.

I pulled my cell phone and called the two people in my life I knew would be there in a heartbeat to stay with me and keep me safe. Together, we are the trifecta. At least that's what we called ourselves.

The first person I called was "Too Tall" Jon, a bouncer and private security agent in the city, who I've known since high school. A quiet guy, confident and humbled, he was the kind of guy you'd want standing next to you in a dark alley in case anything goes down.

Even though Jon said he was on his way, I also called "Big" Joe the Zen master, a bilingual Russian American citizen. We played football in high school together. He is also the type of guy you want next to you if you're in a serious bind. Both of these fellows have always had my back.

When I call, they are only minutes away.

Big Joe arrived first, at what seemed like warp speed. He sat down next to me, and asked, "Hey, you good?"

I simply slid my notebook over to him and said, "Read."

He skimmed the notebook. He could not even finish the second of many pages. His eyes widened, and said, "Ah, I think you need to go to therapy, like now."

I nodded.

Just as Joe and I were discussing how to get me to therapy as quickly as possible, "Too Tall" Jon arrived.

Without a word, Big Joe handed him the pocket-sized notebook. Jon read two sentences and concurred with Joe's opinion.

I needed therapy now.

I asked them if they would hang with me for the day. I didn't want to be alone with my thoughts any longer.

"As soon as you're done with therapy, call me and I will come pick you up, we'll make sure you're good," said Big Joe.

My mental duress became intense as I headed to the mental health clinic. I crossed the street, and watched as cars came to life, trying to swallow me whole.

Buildings, too, took on menacing lifelike characteristics. They were out to get me.

Everywhere I looked, I saw people conjuring up an evil plan for my demise. People who appeared to be walking, smiling, laughing, and talking were really, beneath the facade, plotting ways to harm me. People speaking in different languages were, in my head, only talking in code of their devious plans to assassinate me along with my character.

I turned around and looked at my two best friends, Joe and Jon. I knew them for nearly my entire life.

Yet, I thought they, too, were plotting against me.

I wanted nothing more than to die. At least then I could put an end to this fear and endless suspicion.

Another thought occurred to me: all of my hard and diligent work to get well seemed to amount to nothing. I remembered all of the motivational speaking I had done. For a brief moment, I felt that I could not fail all those people who had told me through letters, e-mails, and Facebook interactions that it was my story that gave them the hope to never die by their own hands.

Once again, however, those old demons crept into my psyche. I thought I beat them years ago. Now they were back to rapidly erode my emotions and my mind. Just like the last three times, they were out for blood. This time, though, I was going to be the person to do something about it.

I opened the clinic's mirrored double doors.

I approached the secretary's window, and without pausing said, "I am late for my therapy session."

The secretary rose and opened the door without another word. She led me to my psychiatrist's office immediately. Perhaps it was the look on my face, or the desperate tone in my voice, that made her act this way.

They sat me down. My whole body felt heavy. My heart was beating slowly and I was breathing deeply, trying to keep myself calm.

My therapist took one look at me and asked, "Kevin, are you thinking of killing yourself?"

Tears huddled in my tear ducts, and then streamed down my face slowly at first, and then more quickly as moments passed. I nodded before saying, "Yes."

She called a doctor into the office with her and they both asked me, simultaneously, "Do you need to go to the hospital?"

"As soon as humanly possible," I said.

My therapist and the doctor described to me what was going to happen next.

I was going to be 5150'd. This would be my fifth time, this time like the fourth time, and like the next two times, I would go willingly.

A 5150 is placing a person into temporary custody who is considered a serious danger to themselves or others. Such a person—me, in this case—is put into a locked-down mental health facility. Then, that person is assessed by a staff consisting of psychiatrists, physicians, therapists, case managers, and social workers.

If a person being 5150'd is identified as a danger to himself (i.e., suicidal), he is put on a twenty-four–hour suicide watch. Every ten to fifteen minutes, the person is checked and asked point blankly, "Do you want to harm yourself?" or "Are you having thoughts of suicide?"

When someone is 5150'd in the city of San Francisco, the police department becomes involved. They are required to handcuff the person. This is California state law. Even though I was consenting to go of my own free will, the clinic has to take steps to ensure the safety of themselves, others, and even me.

I stood against the back of the SFPD's squad car, in plain view of passersby, and obviously in plain view of my favorite cafe that I had frequented for the better part of ten years.

I knew this was not the time to wallow in self-pity or to be filled with embarrassment. This was the time to (as Jon and Joe would say) "Man up! And go balls deep," meaning, handle your business and take care of shit.

And yet, being taken away in handcuffs in front of people who know you because you are such a danger to yourself is not easy.

Four police officers walked into the room, took off their sunglasses, and with one hand at their waist next to their guns, asked, "Do you know why we're here?"

"Yes, to keep me safe," I said.

One of them replied, "Are you thinking of harming anyone?"

"Just myself."

Another officer asked, "Do you want to kill yourself?"

"That's why you were called here."

He explained to me what would transpire. I tried desperately to hold back the tears. I kept them from falling down my face in that particular moment.

The officers patted me down, and asked me if I had any sharp objects in my pockets, like needles or a knife.

"No," I said.

One of them asked me if I did drugs. "Only the ones this clinic prescribes me."

Two officers stood me up and put my hands behind my back, asking me to interlock my two index fingers. They walked me out of the clinic, past the secretary, doctors, therapists, and other patients.

I held my head high, fighting tears.

They opened the double doors of their squad car parked in front of the building. I looked around and saw several people that I knew from the cafe. Other onlookers slowed down and stared.

I was pushed up against the rear of the vehicle, with my head held down. I was handcuffed, extremely tight. It really hurt. I was then asked to place myself in the back seat without help, something I found to be pretty difficult to do without aid or the use of my hands.

I fully understood the drill.

For more than five years, I gave the San Francisco Police Department training at the Golden Gate Club in the Presidio District. Most of that area was owned by Lucas Films, more recently owned by

Disney. Along with a group called Stamp out Stigma and the Mental Health Board, I taught police officers how to better handle a mental health patient when they need to be apprehended or arrested. Stamp out Stigma aims to train all police on how to be empathetic with those who do not have a sound mind and do not understand what they are doing.

After all, those with mental illnesses may not even have a clear idea if they committed a crime let alone what crime they have committed. A panel of five or six of us worked with twenty to fifty police officers. Our job was to make these officers aware of what different mental illnesses may look like, and how they can assess who is or is not dangerous. I taught them about bipolar disorder, as I lived through it, and I educated them on my disease's severity. Every year it seemed that the policemen and women were eager to learn and glad to be reeducated. They seemed better off after our presentation. In fact, they felt empowered now that they had a better understanding of what those with a brain illness deal with every day. Some speakers had more difficult and painful experiences with police officers in the past. We also helped the officers realize who was to be taken to a psychiatric unit as opposed to those who needed to be incarcerated.

Patricia, a great friend and colleague of mine, and the current Executive Director of the San Francisco Mental Health Board (a board I sat on for three years) organized and executed the entire event alongside Officer Mike. Together they made it all happen each year. The program has since been cut, due to lack of funding, but during its run several officers were trained, and they took that newly found knowledge and spread it across the police department.

On the ride to Psychiatric Emergency Services, I said to the police officers who handcuffed and escorted me, "I didn't realize how uncomfortable handcuffs truly were."

The two officers smirked.

Down the road, I told the officers how sorry I was for making them come out to the clinic and transport me.

They said they were thankful that I did not put up a fight.

As the car rolled to a stop, I saw a familiar face outside my left window. It was a student with whom I had worked when I had the job at San Francisco's School of the Arts. That particular student was now a

City College of San Francisco Student; he walked slowly in front of the car, and peered in.

It was obvious to me that he recognized me immediately.

He looked right into my eyes, possibly thinking, Kevin Hines, no way! I knew then that the entire student body of SOTA and the staff would soon hear the news. I also knew that the rumors would spread like wildfire and explode into some crazy story about me going to prison for a crime I didn't commit. Most of the staff at SOTA knew of my mental health difficulties, but I certainly did not want them thinking I was a criminal. Either way it was a glimpse into what people might say, and it was forgotten as soon as I got to the ward.

The ride was quick. We pulled into hospital's main drop-off access.

The officers opened my door and thanked me for my calm and collected attitude. They asked me how they did, according to the trainings I had been giving.

I said they were great.

With an officer on either side of me, I entered the Psychiatric Emergency Services building. My handcuffs were soon removed and the police officers admitted me, filled out some paperwork, shook my hand, and wished me the best of luck.

Shortly after my arrival, I watched as the nurses and doctors yelled out, "Code Blue! Code Blue, need a crash cart ASAP!" An elderly patient collapsed to the floor while squeezing his chest in cardiac arrest.

Then nurses shouted out, "He has no pulse!"

I watched as they administered CPR before the crash cart arrived, reviving the man.

I sat, watching and waiting for the day to calm down for the staff.

When the room emptied of cardiac arrests and other acute traumas, a nurse asked if I wanted any food.

I shook my head "no." Food was the last thing on my mind: I was breathing rapidly and felt extremely paranoid and delusional. I fought off the rapid thoughts as diligently as I could. I was given Ativan to calm my nerves and stop my psychosis.

Hours went by before I was informed that I would be transported to another hospital. When the ambulance arrived, I was strapped in, transported, and locked down.

I experienced good, bad, and just plain ugly experiences at the amazingly equipped and odd smelling third floor lockdown psych unit at the hospital. The smell can only be detected by those first coming in, it blends into normalcy after a few days of being there. In the beginning, while psychosis still ran through my veins, I screamed, ran into my room threw my furniture up and sideways, and exclaimed, "They are here, they are coming to kill me. Protect yourselves!!"

I was sporadic, screaming at the top of my lungs, and frantic. I believed that the ubiquitous "they" were out to get me, that they were out for blood, and that no one could be trusted. My breakdown was a large-scale paranoid delusion. The orderlies were called in, and once again I found security guards at my door. The nurses behind them were ready to hold me down and administer a tranquilizer. This time was like my third hospitalization all over again, the only difference was that this time my fists were not bloody from beating my room's wall. Thankfully, medication technology had changed since that third time in the ward. This being the fifth time Dr. Mel, my pal, rushed into the room and said, "Ask him if he will take a pill form of the drug, you do not have to inject him." They asked and I obliged. The pill tranquilizer was administered. I would soon calm down and my muscles would be safe from deep injection.

One day soon after my furniture incident, one of my great buddies, Chris, and my wife came to see me. I was under the influence of heavy sedatives and simultaneously in a massive manic episode. Prior to my hospitalization, the two of them shared a running joke that made this next scenario even more hilarious. Chris calls himself my wife's secret lover, and they both give me shit about it all the time when I am well.

When Chris and my wife arrived, the hospital fire alarm sounded, according to Chris.

I don't remember what happened next. Chris told me I barricaded myself behind two tables, flipping them onto their sides and blockading the tables with four chairs. Then, I pulled Chris in close and said, "Chris, I am going to be in here for the rest of my life. You have to take care of my wife."

He said. "You'll be out soon—don't worry."

I wasn't having any of it. "They'll never let me out of here! I give you permission to marry her, keep her safe!" There was a strain in my voice—the kind that comes from the desperation and sadness you inevitably feel when you know you're on the verge of losing something, someone, important. I believed I was staying in that hospital for the rest of my life. My actions, my voice, and my mind all said so.

I would find wellness again.

That, though, seemed unfathomable to me.

These kinds of scenarios are all too familiar for my family, close friends, and me.

Complete psychosis.

But that story was getting old. Everyone—most of all, me—was tired of it.

Back and forth I went, in and out of the psych wards. I had been stuck in those H-shaped halls before, many a time.

When out of the hospital, back on what we hoped would be the right meds for me, I exercised rigorously, found healthy eating habits and a great sleep pattern, and read important educational reading material as to the newest findings on my disease. Along with that, I spent copious amounts of time reflecting with my wife, as well as my therapists. I also went to church every Sunday with my wife, and my faith was strong, is strong. I am no preacher but these are the tools that help me get through each day.

I was so much better now. I was able this time around to know that I wanted to get well, that this was just another episode that would pass. I knew that every day I woke up was a good day, another day to try again, to get right again. No matter what a person's lot in life, a new day offers a new opportunity to move forward, to put the past behind, and to surpass any obstacle in their way.

Sometimes, I still catch myself staring in the mirror at the twenty-three-staple scar on my side. Not a pretty sight, it serves as a constant reminder of that day and how far I have come.

I have lived for more than a decade since the day I was supposed to die.

I have been given a coveted second chance at life.

This scar now reminds me of a promise more powerful than the memory of that jump ten years ago. It's the promise that I'll have myself hospitalized due to psychosis in a heartbeat, every time I feel those old demons rise to the surface of my mind again.

I understand, now more than ever, too much is at stake. Too many people love me dearly. Too many people depend on me.

My life is not mine to take in the first place.

These days, I am healthily addicted to keeping physically fit, as well as mentally stable. I run four to six miles a day. Sometimes I take my beautiful golden Shar Pei, Max, with his football jersey-looking blond shoulder stripes and smelly wrinkly folds along with me. However, my absolute favorite route to run is the one where I have to leave Max at home. He doesn't like being left behind but I've found that he doesn't handle long distances very well.

The route is simple: I start at one of San Francisco's main thoroughfares, 19th and Holloway, next to San Francisco State's manicured campus. From there, I run the full length of 19th Avenue, to 19th and Irving along the City streets that are an endlessly interesting mix of urban landscape, the shade of trees, the sounds of cars and of people, running as I do, or walking to or from their homes. The entire length of 19th Avenue is exactly six miles there and back—or, in my case, 8,989 steps.

I ran that route the night I decided to place this story at the end of my book.

As I ran back my legs were spinning so fast it was like I had wheels. I doubt too many people could even see my legs.

OK, that last part is a bit of an exaggeration, but that's how I felt. Like I was running so fast I might as well be flying. Nothing could stop me. Then, an enormous white quad-cab construction work truck pulled out of the driveway in front of me, blocking my path.

The truck was filled with rough-looking, hardhat wearing workmen of various ethnicities. As they pulled out into traffic, a funny thing happened.

I started to run again, passing the truck which hadn't quite started driving yet. The workers saw me coming, with my black tank top on, and my arms and legs hustling as fast as I could to climb up that hill.

When I turned to look at the lot of them, they were yelling something at me. I could not hear anything because, as always when I run, my iPod Nano was playing my favorite "pump-me-up" running song. The song was by a band called Friends of Emmet (a band from Dublin, Ireland). Earlier that year the band contacted my manager to tell me that they wrote a beautiful song about my life story. The song was called "Coming Apart." I was actually one of the first people in the public to ever hear it. After meeting two band members in Los Angeles that year, I had it on my MP3 player and listened to it constantly. The song is relatable to anyone with suicidal thoughts, or even those who love someone who is. Most of the band lives in Dublin, Ireland, and one member of the band, Mark Leddy, lives in Los Angeles. It was he and bassist Keith Geraghty that reached out to me and shared that honor. I believe the song will someday reach out to millions, as the band has made suicide prevention their personal cause.

The song was on repeat and at full volume (probably the reason I am having a hard time hearing people's low spoken voices in general) while I was on my typical six to nine mile run. I looked at the construction crew I passed.

It was as if they had just seen their favorite Hollywood actor.

These fellows could have cared less about any actor in the Hollywood Hills. I raised my right arm and gave them my old favorite sign. It was my index finger touching my thumb and my other three fingers raised to a solute. If I did that in Brazil, it would have been an entirely different scenario, in Brazil the very same hand sign is a sign of disrespect, but since I was in the city by the Bay, it was all good. They were still yelling something, but I kept running.

I kept my short wrestling legs moving as fast as my cross-training Under Armour kicks could take me. Then I looked up and about fifteen yards away, the next block's light turned green. I was more determined than ever to make that light. My heart pumped and my head filled with endorphins as I sprinted like lightning.

This time, I really did have wheels. With two seconds left on the green walk light, I was ten yards off, running like a gazelle, my strides becoming wider and wider; with one second left, the light turned red as my right foot touched the curb.

I made it. What a rush.

I kept moving, running like a savage beast, as my high school buddies would have said. There was no time for a sigh of relief. I just wanted to make it home in record time.

About three blocks down, I heard honking through my earphones. I turned and sure enough, those same construction workers and their gigantic truck pulled to the side, blocking traffic at a green light. They yelled at me and at the same time, honked the horn. I took my left earphone out of my ear. The dude in the right passenger seat looked at me with awe and yells out, "You jumped the Golden Gate!!" He must have seen me on Larry King, or in the film *The Bridge*, or my appearance in 2009 on *20/20* with John Stossel. No matter how they knew my story, however, they knew about my struggle with mental wellness—they knew about my desire to spread awareness for suicide prevention.

Since 2001, I have been extremely public about my mental illness, my jump, and my healing. I decided to grant the *San Francisco Examiner* my first interview. The article was called "Instant Regret." Since then I have been a pundit on national and international media outlets, including *Larry King*, *20/20*, Ireland's famed *Tonight with Vincent Browne*, *Good Morning America*, the documentary film by Eric Steel, called *The Bridge* about the deaths on the Golden Gate Bridge in 2004 which was released at the Tribeca Film Festival. Alongside the media work I have done to promote suicide prevention and raising a rail or net at the Golden Gate Bridge.

After the construction worker yelled out of his truck, "You jumped the Golden Gate!" I was stunned, but replied kindly, "Yeah, I did."

Everyone in the truck started hollering and bustling within the quad cab. They seemed amazed that I could, after having a broken back from the jump, and after having a metal plate and cage replace my vertebrae, walk, let alone run. The guy in the passenger looked like his eyes were popping out of his head. In some way, they were proud to have come across me.

Looking back at that moment, I realized something.

I am a native San Franciscan. Those guys were the true meaning and epitome of the city. They are what make this city tick, those six to eight hard-working, blue collar, potentially weekend bar drinking, all-out brawling, throw-down-for-their-brothers-in-a-heartbeat, kind of fellas. Judging by their looks, these guys had seen it all. I will most likely never run into that particular group again. If I ever do, I am going to thank them for making my day. They inspired me to keep up everything I was doing without even knowing it.

In my mind's eye, I looked back to my most recent mental relapse and psychiatric stay that occurred a little more than a month before writing these pages. I realized, once again, that no matter how hard life gets, you just gotta "keep on keeping on." When I got home, I told my wife what happened over dinner. She said, "That's great, honey. See how far you've come?"

Those guys left me with a feeling of empowerment, a feeling I have not enjoyed in quite a while. Who knows? Maybe one or all of them had seen the film, *The Bridge*. What became even more obvious about the workmen was the fact that they seemed to really appreciate my struggle and hope for a good outcome.

They saw that I had found success. Not the monetary kind, but the kind that comes from living life to the fullest extent. For that moment in time, for one brief period, I had a profound experience. I pushed my general paranoia and painful depression aside. I felt a rush of positivity. I remembered that I have a purpose on this earth and that purpose is to continue my work of prevention and living mentally well every day.

I can do it. We can all do it. We can live well with a mental illness most days. And the days we have a hard time, we can remember what the good times are like and that with a great deal of effort we can always survive and that no one suffering mentally has to die by suicide. With every pain-filled moment a lesson is to be learned. Life isn't easy, no one ever said it would be. Every single person on the planet has challenges to overcome. It is what makes this world so fantastic. We can face such challenges and triumph over adversity. We can win the game of life. I know I will always battle back from the brink, I will always win, I will always heal, I will always fight for my wellness. It was not like this my whole life. I jumped off that bridge in the midst of great desperation and the belief that I had no other option. There is always another option, life is that option, life is worth living, and we must remember tomorrow is not today. It is also my belief that everyone on the planet has his or her own purpose. It is up to each individual to determine whether it is a positive, productive one.

What a feeling of triumph this encounter with the construction workers gave me. After the chance meeting with my new friends, I sprinted the rest of the way home with a newfound energy.

My mom and dad said it best: "Life is what you make it." At that second, a specific scene in the great Peter Sellers movie *Being There* rang true in my head. It was the scene after the simple gardener Chance,

Sellers' character, dies. A businessman at his funeral said, "Life is but a state of mind."

I never heard it repeated, and quite frankly, I never heard a statement that would end up meaning so much to me. However, I do know life is not a Hollywood movie. It is real and it can swallow you whole, tear you apart, and spit you out. It is completely up to you to pick yourself up, dust yourself off, and start all over again. The key in my life was my realization that I held the power to change my present struggles into a successful future.

The dreams of my future have become crystal clear. I know that dying by my own hands is never the answer—no matter what situation faces me. I know that by fighting every day to stay well, I walk the path God has laid out for me. He saved me when I was sure to die. There is nothing in my life more profound than that. If I were to die by suicide now, all of the people I have met, cared for, helped or loved would be crushed until the end of their lives. If I die by suicide now, what about all of the audiences with students and adults alike who have contemplated suicide, to which I have spoken about suicide prevention and staying mentally healthy? How would such an action affect each of their lives?

They could potentially think, "If he couldn't live, then how can I?" That's dangerous. It is also a huge weight on my shoulders, but one I am prepared, willing, and able to carry. The people who have come up to me in every state or country in which I have spoken, and said, "I was going to kill myself, but because of you and your speech, now I will not," depend on me in some small way to stay alive and well. That is exactly what I plan to do, no matter how bad it gets or what mental breakdowns I experience from here on. I will stay alive.

I will keep on keepin' on.

CHAPTER 15

~

A Decade of Change

If you want to know the truth, I originally thought that speaking publicly—telling my story—was a ridiculous idea. Yet, in 2011—eleven years after I attempted to take my own life by suicide—I found myself staring at a large audience at Iowa State University. Minutes before I was going to take the stage, I could hear the murmur of voices and the shuffling of chairs from behind the curtain. As I listened to the crowd that had gathered to hear me speak, I couldn't help but reflect on how far I'd come. From the beginning of my suffering, I had no clear vision about how to find my inner voice to say nothing of my public one. A big part of my journey was realizing that we must all find it eventually. And when we do, it becomes our duty that we look out for those who were hurting and in pain.

Likewise, if you have a voice that you are willing to share with the public, one you think expresses great healing, maturing, and leaves thoughts in the minds of those listening to find help, you should use it.

We are all "our brothers' and sisters' keepers."

We are on this planet to lead and give back whenever and wherever we can. If everyone shared her inspiring life story, I know for a fact that so many of us can and will change people's lives for the better.

Over the past eleven years, I was presented with many awards and accolades for my efforts as a public speaker and mental health advocate.

Although I never expected to be a public speaker, it nonetheless became validation for my existence that—before—had been fraught with so much pain and distress. I began to believe that my life was worth living. Not because of the awards, not even because of the speeches, but because of the wellness and inner peace I achieved by helping others find their mental well-being. Helping people has become second nature to me. I now realize how true the statement that "life is a gift" really is. I am blessed; this new lease on life is meant for more than just sitting around watching cable TV, eating potato chips, and drinking diet cola. My purpose opened for me and I grabbed ahold of it with all I had.

I gave so much of myself so each audience member could finally find happiness (I hoped). Who knew a story could mean so much to so many people? There are times where I doubt its power today, until another soul tells me how it changed their life for the better, or how my story prompted them to seek professional help to begin the process of living mentally well.

Or, maybe it isn't my story—after all, every person's story is relevant. Every triumph over adversity experience in some small way can be shared for the betterment of the rest of us. I'm grateful to have the opportunity, though, to share what I know of happiness and life. Goodness knows it could have turned out differently.

I'm standing on a stage at Iowa State University today because nine years after my attempt, I was given the opportunity to join a socially conscious speaker's bureau. I signed up with The Parsons Company, Inc., which is a talent management agency that cares about the social issues of our time, like grief and loss, alcohol and drug prevention, anti-bullying, veterans' rights, active duty military aid, and suicide prevention.

Today, though, I began by speaking at the Iowa City Crisis Center at a function meant to reach out to families in crisis. The Iowa City Crisis Center is a half food bank and half crisis hotline, providing mental health services to the surrounding communities. My "driver" from the airport to the crisis center, Kelly, was the director at the Crisis Center. Kelly is the reason I had the pleasure of coming to Iowa in the first place.

When I began public speaking, Kelly heard about my presentation and story. She wanted me to present at the Crisis Center in Johnson

City. We spoke on the phone prior to the trip. She informed me that she had worked on my arrival for several years now with Phyllis, my manager from the Parsons Company, and the speaker's bureau. Kelly said that it was an honor to have me in her town for such a pertinent reason.

My job: to present at 1:00 p.m. that day to a "hodgepodge" (as she so eloquently put it in Iowa terms during our ride into town from the airport) of individuals and families. Members of the audience would be suffering with their own mental struggles, while others were family members, and even more were clinicians in the field of suicide awareness and prevention. A large mix of NAMI (National Alliance on Mental Illness) Iowa City members would be present.

What would happen that day, though, was unexpected. But then again, when you take the stage as a public speaker, sometimes all you can expect is the unexpected.

At Iowa State University, the room was packed. The capacity was eighty people, but about 110 shuffled into the space, standing along the walls since the seats had long since been filled. Extra chairs needed to be found and placed. Yet, despite the large number of attendees, it was also an intimate setting: the stage wasn't so high as to make me feel distant. I would be speaking to a few more than a hundred of my newest friends.

After my ninety-minute presentation, the audience gave me a standing ovation and a man would approach me whose son had Tourettes. The man would embrace me in a tear-filled hug, telling me that my story changed his life.

A line formed near the door, filled with other people who were personally touched by my story and many others who stated that they were greatly affected by my presentation. The last person in line who waited to talk to me approached. She was a visibly troubled young lady in a pink tank top and a blue bandana. She was in tears, she was in pain.

She was, by the look in her eyes, lost.

She had come to the event alone, though she admitted to me that she did not know if she would have the courage to show up at all. She had been hearing voices telling her she was useless, and that she had to die. She saw things only visible to her. We had much in common. She believed that suicide was her destiny. I did my best to convince her otherwise. Her voice cracked as she spoke to me.

Tears quickly crawled down her face as she told me that hospitalization was no option for her psychosis because her family was still paying off her last visit to a psychiatric unit.

By now, tears streamed down her face, even though it was obvious that she tried to hold them back. She said she had been battling depression, most specifically bipolar disorder, for more than ten years.

Her suicidal ideations began in grade school.

I asked her if she was suicidal right then. Her whisper of a voice went from cracking and waning to a brief silence. Then she shook her head, *no*. "I just don't know what to do. I am so tired of fighting this disease. I hate it. I am in so much pain." She continued, telling me that she felt destroyed because of this depression and her distorted reality. Seeing and hearing things that no one else can acknowledge or even understand.

As she spoke, I started to cry, too. Her experiences—so close to my own—resonated with my memory of feeling utterly lost and hopeless.

I hear stories like this everywhere I travel and speak. The stories make an unforgettable impression inside my heart and head. The stories can have a tendency to rattle me. I try not to internalize stories like this, but how can I not, at least just a little bit? I have always had the gift and the curse of being able to feel others' emotions.

Today was no exception. She said she had been abused as a child. She started to cry so hard it was difficult to understand what she was saying. I told her she deserved to be here among the rest of us. I did my best to focus and give her my most sound thoughts and ideas as to how she could keep up the fight and stay in this life. I told this young woman that her life was a gift, even though her brain was telling her otherwise. I told her that she was needed.

"You are loved and people care about your well-being," I said. But, I felt that my consoling words fell on deaf ears. I kept talking to her, though. I kept telling her she was needed and loved, that her life was worth more than any one person could ever imagine.

Eventually, she perked up, her crying quieted.

Wiping the tears from her cheeks, she thanked me and told me how much my presentation was personally needed. We shook hands and I put my left hand over both of our right hands and said, "You can do this. You got this!"

She nodded and somberly walked away.

The technician came in to disconnect my computer, and I placed it in my laptop bag. I gathered my other odds and ends, speaking to Kelly one last time, and prepared for my trip to the airport. As I was gathering my belongings, another event official approached us. The look on her face was stern and serious. "There's a girl in a tank top with a bandana in the women's restroom crying."

Kelly, a trained counselor and social worker, had already gone in to help. The Director stated that she had gone to the restroom and found the young lady slumped to the floor, absolutely beside herself.

A half hour passed. I was nervous and sick to my stomach with fear. I waited in the hallway with every awful emotion surfacing in me while I waited for another update. Waiting, while thinking of all the possible outcomes. I knew who was in the restroom.

Another fifteen minutes passed. I kept looking in the direction of the restroom door. Every noise, creak, or slam of a door captured my full attention.

Finally, I couldn't take the suspense any more. I asked the director if she would go in and see if everything was all right. She nodded and pushed open the heavy wooden door that slapped shut behind her. Another minute, then a light laughter chirped from under the restroom's door.

I sighed in relief.

Kelly, the director and the young woman started laughing because of me. I was so concerned but could not enter the ladies' room.

The young woman left the restroom. She looked straight at me, tears still flowing down her face. We embraced one more time. I put my hands on her shoulders. "You got this! You are going to get well. It's going to take a great deal of hard work but it is going to happen. You deserve to live well."

She nodded her head in agreement. Then, she broke down again. Thoughts of suicide were enveloping her brain. Kelly had convinced her that another hospital bill was well worth it, if it meant that she would be safe and if it meant she would live.

I told her a short story, one I share with very few people. When I used to be in situations close to her current dilemma, I would go to my bathroom, look directly into my mirror and say, "I love you, Kevin

Hines. You are a good man, a good human being, and you deserve to live. No matter what the inner voices tell you. You must stay here. You are loved."

I shortened it for her and said to simply look in front of any mirror and either in your head or aloud recite these words: "I love you [fill in your own name]." I told her she should do this every day. I said to her that she would be surprised at how quickly she was going to learn to believe it.

The next day, as I was getting ready to leave for the airport, I got a call from Kelly. Kelly told me that the young woman who had approached me after the event was in a psychiatric hospital, working on her mental health. She was there for a change in scenery, or rather, a change in her life—a change for the better.

No one wants to go to psychiatric hospitals; no one wants to stay there. But they can be an oasis in a desert of mental despair. They can provide comfort, safety, and care during the worst of times. They can be a place of beginnings—beginning to heal, to see the light, to be well.

Later, I was made aware that she was safe and that Iowa's mental health services are taking good care of her. I felt a rush of relief come over me. We had done great work.

We had changed her course. We had saved a life.

Immediately after the presentation at Iowa State, I was driven to the airport so I could catch the next flight to Knoxville, Tennessee, for another presentation at the University of Tennessee. And from there, I would fly to Dublin, Ireland. This was no vacation, however. The all-Irish American band Friends of Emmet had booked me for a speaking event in Ireland to help raise awareness about suicide. The rate of deaths due to suicide are also on the rise in Ireland as in the United States. In Ireland, however, the suicide rate for men ages fifteen to twenty-four has been increasing at an alarming rate.

I would be interviewed on a nationally broadcast television show *Tonight with Vincent Browne* as an advocate for suicide prevention. This, after flying across the United States for several speaking events.

On the plane ride to Ireland, I sat next to a quiet and soft-spoken Irishman. As I buckled my seatbelt, I noticed he was reading the Irish *Economic Times*. Always the talker, I asked the man, "Do you work in finance?"

He looked up from his magazine and nodded. I told him that my dad has worked as a banker in San Francisco for thirty-five years. His expression shifted into a smile, and he asked what I did.

"I'm a public speaker," I told him. When he asked what I spoke about, I told him my story and then explained my relationship to the band Friends of Emmet and their mission to spread awareness of suicide prevention in Ireland.

The man told me that he had experienced a suicide in his family, too.

"Kevin," he said, "I'll be watching you on *Tonight with Vincent Browne*. I watch that show every weekday night anyway."

Awaiting my arrival was Friends of Emmets' Keith Geraghty, the band's bassist. At his side was Phil Dargon, one of the gentlemen partially responsible for the creation of Friends of Emmet.

I went to Ireland because Ireland is light years behind other leading countries in terms of suicide prevention. My interview with Vincent Browne would begin the tour. If you don't know, Vincent Browne is to Ireland what Piers Morgan or Larry King is to the United States. Such a popular show, it's rumored the president of Ireland herself watches the show every night.

This would be the first time I would be interviewed on suicide prevention for a full forty minutes live on a nationally broadcast show. The host, Mr. Browne, and his producers were certainly taking a risk covering a topic like suicide prevention because it wasn't a topic normally covered in the Irish news. The number of suicides that year, though, made it evidently clear that the risk was worth every Euro spent on the production.

The glare of the camera light was in my eyes and Mr. Browne asked me about my personal experience with suicide. And about my message of mental wellness. As I spoke, viewers began to tweet.

They tweeted their support for the broadcast.

They tweeted shortened versions of their personal stories.

Tweets came in by the hundreds about the show and its impact on the country.

Write-ups from my interview on *Tonight with Vincent Browne* covered the front pages of the *Irish Mirror*, *Westmeath Examiner*, and the *Irish Times*. The joint goal of Friends of Emmet and I were nearly realized: we practically reached the entire country. We could not walk the streets of Ireland without being approached and thanked for bringing the topics of mental health and suicide to the nation's attention.

After watching the interview, the youngest son of a local Irish family tweeted into the show asking for our help. The bassist, Keith Geraghty, asked if the family would be meet with him and me at a hotel in Dublin. Though it was a three-hour drive from their home, this family wanted to talk about their experience with suicide. They also needed closure.

At first, the father was quiet, as though he was heartbroken.

The youngest son—the one who had tweeted into the show—told us how he found his older brother hanging from a rafter in the home.

After the son finished speaking, the father looked up from his hands, he said, in a quiet voice, "We haven't told anybody this." Even the priest covered the cause of death up for the family since the real reason would have caused the family additional and undue pain.

Yet, they said our outspoken approach to these serious and difficult issues inspired their family to talk openly again. They wanted to talk about suicide, but in a community that encouraged silence on the issue, they never knew how to get their message out to the public.

Then the youngest son spoke again, "We need to talk about this, as a nation. We can't keep calling them 'accidental deaths.'"

We said goodnight to the family and wished them well.

I later heard that the youngest son would begin his own fight for raising awareness of suicide in Ireland. He has his own story to tell; his own wisdom about the necessity of mental wellness. I might be just a small part of that; it's like I said: stories are powerful. It's what we do with them that makes a difference.

It hasn't been easy. Every morning I wake up next to my wife is a good day. Every morning that I roll over and see my wife amazes me.

I should have died when I jumped from the Golden Gate Bridge. Instead, though, I lived. And for that I am eternally grateful.

I have learned that I will I struggle daily with my version of bipolar disorder. I don't always win each match but I will always get up off the mat, doing all that I can to live mentally well. The catastrophic pain I regularly endure is due to a brain disease that eases its symptoms with treatment. This is true for everyone who has bipolar disorder.

Suicide has never been the solution to any problem.

The pain and struggle will pass after a great deal of hard work and effort to live mentally well.

I can't let God, my family, or myself down.

This time, I will succeed.

This time, I will thrive.

This time and every time I will survive.

You will, too.

Good journey to you and yours. Stay here. Stay well. Stay alive. I promise that I will do exactly the same.

The Art of Living Mentally Well—Most Days

A Quick Guide to Learning How to Live and Stay Mentally Well

KEVIN HINES,
WITH DR. DANIEL J. REIDENBERG,
PsyD, FAPA, FACFEI, CRS, BCPC, CMT
EXECUTIVE DIRECTOR OF SAVE

My name is Kevin Hines and I have a severe mental illness. I am not a licensed mental health clinician—but I am living well most days while having a mental disorder. At age seventeen, I was diagnosed with bipolar disorder. Years later it would be narrowed down to bipolar type 1, with psychotic features. I suffered greatly from extreme paranoia, terrible depressions, awful manic highs, and hallucinations, auditory and visual, as well as panic attacks.

My family took me to doctors and the doctors prescribed treatments—but one day, unable to bear the pain, I believed I had to kill myself. I went to the Golden Gate Bridge and jumped. Yes, I jumped. I fell 220 feet—approximately twenty-five stories—at 75 mph. The fall took four seconds. Those seconds changed my life forever.

Thankfully, I survived. My story is nothing short of miraculous.

I'm so grateful to still be alive, although I still struggle to live mentally well. I am one of the 57 million adult Americans who suffer with a mental illness. I have now made it my life's work to educate people all over this great country, and around the globe, to prevent suicide and understand mental illnesses.

I will tell you now that it takes hard work to get well. It takes hard work to stay well. Most of the time, I am healthy and happy. Some days are difficult.

The information in this handbook is not clinically proven advice. The advice in this manual is based on my long personal experience with managing dipolar disorder. All information in this section refers to personal suggestions based on what has worked for me.

I have no academic or professional experience as a healthcare provider. I have a personal account of suffering greatly from extreme paranoia, terrible depressions, awful manic highs, auditory and visual hallucinations, and panic attacks, and finding hope in the process and learning the art of living mentally well.

Complete Ten Steps Daily to Begin Learning the Art of Living Mentally Well

I live with bipolar disorder and by following this very strict routine of specific steps, I stay focused and mentally well most days.

1. **Therapy.** I participate in cognitive behavioral therapy ("talk therapy"), meditation, and some other modern therapies. (Some people only need a single type of therapy, but many of us need to use several types.)
2. **Medication.** I take my medication with 100 percent accuracy at the same time every day.
3. **Exercise.** Routine cardiovascular or strength training exercises are helpful because of the endorphins released from the body. For me, running is effective.
4. **Sleep.** I control my circadian rhythm; I get seven to eight hours of sleep most nights. Sufficient sleep is essential for wellness, combined with these other steps.
5. **Food.** To heal mentally, you need a healthy diet. After all, your brain is part of the body you're feeding! I eat good, nutritious foods most of the time.
6. **Education.** I keep myself educated about my disorder—and I educate my family and friends, too.
7. **Refrain from using alcohol.** I don't drink alcohol. Drinking if you have a mental illness further weakens your brain's ability to function properly. Drinking if you take medications can change

how the medications work (decreasing or increasing their effects), which can seriously harm you.

8. **Refrain from using recreational drugs.** I don't use recreational drugs, either, for the same reasons I don't drink alcohol.

9. **Coping.** I have good and positive coping mechanisms to deal with the stress of my everyday symptoms. That includes spending time with people who care about me. There are many ways to cope: with friends, with a pet, with a hobby, or through religious practices.

10. **My Binder.** I created an "Emergency Mental Health Binder," or an eFile. I recommend you put one together, too.

If you think following these **10 Steps** sounds like hard work—well, go re-read through all my symptoms! That "routine" was a million times worse! This routine might be tough but by following it my life is good.

The Emergency Mental Health Binder/eFile

I created a binder/eFile to help my family and friends know what to expect and what to do if I need help.

I suggest you create copies of your binder for each of your Personal Protectors. (My family and doctors hold copies of my binder.) Talk to each person before giving them a binder. Be sure they are supportive, understanding people who have the courage to make decisions for you, if you are incapable.

Your Personal Protectors
People in my life—the people who truly care about me or who spend significant time with me—have a copy of the binder.

Make a list. Here are some people to consider in your life:

Your parents or legal guardians, or those in a parental role to you (maybe your best friend's parents, or an aunt or uncle).
Your closest friends
Your spouse, or girlfriend or boyfriend

Therapist

Psychiatrist

Case Manager or Social Worker

School principal, counselor or coach

Priest, pastor, rabbi, imam or spiritual advisor

Start there.

If you feel more people should have a copy, and those people are willing to take on this responsibility, by all means create more binders.

Binder Contents

Here are sections you want to include in each binder/eFile:

Name, address, e-mail address, and direct phone number of your personal emergency contacts. (Preferably between two to seven people.)

Name, address, e-mail address, and direct phone number of your psychiatrist, your therapist, and your spiritual advisor.

The name, definition, and signs of your particular mental disorder or mental health issue.

The medications you take dosage and time to take them.

Common symptoms of your condition, so each Personal Protector can watch for them.

A list of triggers that affect your mental state, such as:

Reaction to alcohol

Foods that affect you badly

"Friends" you should avoid

Time you should go home, go to bed

Phobias or uncomfortable environments

Phrases you might use to express suicidal thoughts, such as: "I just hate living," or "I don't belong here," or "I want to die."

Any of these, and similar phrases, are clear warnings that your Protector must take action for your personal safety!

This binder has worked well for me. My Personal Protectors appreciate having this information. I hope it will help you!

When You Feel Suicidal

If you are having suicidal thoughts, the more time you give yourself without an attempt to hurt yourself, the better chance you have of staying alive.

Tell yourself: "I won't do anything for a few days, maybe even a week or two."

This time allows for more rational thought to enter into your mind.

Take this time to seek out and find mental health help!

Find supportive people to spend time with.

Speak up! Tell someone you trust about your thoughts.

Enter regular in-patient treatment.

Realize that being admitted to a psychiatric hospital might be a good thing. It might keep you alive! Make plans and take action. Let family and friends know that they must admit you, if they fear for your life.

Suicide is never a solution.

Suicide is never a solution to any problem. Period.

What I Believe about Me—And about You

I Believe That . . .

I am here for a reason. I believe each of us is here for a purpose. Mine is to help those with thoughts of suicide, and to help those with any mental health issues or disorders find a better solution to their temporary mental pain. I am here to help those in need find hope for a beautiful future.

I believe you can learn the signs of suicidal ideation and planning, so you can help yourself and those you love avoid pain and suffering. Take care of your own mental health first before going to the aid of others in similar situations.

I also believe that if I had been in a healthy state of mind during my teen years, I would never have made a suicide attempt. Even with bi-polar disorder, if I had followed my treatment plan, I would most likely not have attempted suicide.

Get on track with a treatment plan now. Follow it 100 percent. Do not wait in denial.

Speak up! Get help and get it now. To find a doctor who is right for you and your mental state, you need help from your personal protectors, who can do the homework to find you the right care.

Get out and fight that discrimination! Don't let others mock or trivialize people with mental health issues.

I believe that my doctor should have told me what I desperately needed to hear:

My great emotional pain would not be permanent.

Almost all of people who suffer the way I did get better with treatment.

With a very strict routine, I could live well with my brain disease.

Because I had bipolar disorder, I should never use alcohol or recreational drugs or while taking prescription medications.

Consult with your doctor! Find a specialist who takes the time to inform and educate his patients.

I believe I should have not kept beating myself up over "spilled milk." Or, as my grandfather used to say, "Don't sweat the small stuff." Forgive yourself for any wrongs you feel you've done.

I believe that I am not alone.

I believe that you are not alone!

Do you think no one cares? You are wrong: I care.

There Is Hope, That's My Motto

There is hope.

No matter how dismal any experience, I believe that around any dark corner there is more than just a glimmer of light. I hope reading about my personal journey, and how I handle my disease, has been some advantage to you.

There is no cure. I still battle depression, and I even still have thoughts of suicide. I still have all of the symptoms that I had in my worst days. The difference is that I have been given the tools to reduce my symptoms, to find and keep wellness.

I function well, because I understand and use these tools to break the cycle of Bipolar Disorder. I now live a good life! Since my jump and subsequent recovery, I met the love of my life and got married.

We have a home in California. I have also been blessed to work for major suicide prevention and mental health organizations throughout the country. I work daily with some of the greatest and most innovative minds in both fields, which is such a gift to me.

Life, I now believe is the single greatest gift that we have ever been given. I take no one thing for granted anymore.

When one has been given a second chance at life as I have, one must live every day like it matters most.

Mindfulness helps me stay in the present, focused on achievable goals and aspirations.

I am so glad to have this gift, and I want to share it with all of you.

Side Bar for Clinicians

Your patient is a human, not a condition. Let them know that they, too, are a valuable and important being on this earth. They have a purpose!

Shift your patients them away from labeling themselves bipolar, or schizophrenic, or mentally ill. That's not who they are. That's a condition they have. Teach them to say "I have bipolar disorder," not "I am bipolar." That is a disease; it is not their identity.

Peer to peer interaction is so important as well. Help your clients find others who are like them, with similar disorders, or illnesses, and similar problems.

I have been blessed—not only to have a second chance at life, but so many chances at good mental health. After being dragged into the darkness of my own mind, and enduring depression's physical pain, I was given a second chance at life. It's a life I will never take for granted again, one that I will never risk losing by my own hands.

Help and Hope on the Internet

You can find answers to your questions, and more information about suicide prevention and mental health issues at these websites:

Living Mentally Well with Kevin Hines: www.facebook.com/pages/
Living-Mentally-Well-with-Kevin-Hines/136317109723674

Suicide Awareness Voices of Education: www.save.org
National Suicide Prevention Lifeline: www.suicidepreventionlifeline
.org; 1-800-273-8255. Press #1 for Veterans/Active Military
www.KevinHinesStory.com: Yes, that's my website! You can leave
me a message!

Remember, it's OK not to be OK—but more importantly remember everyone needs help sometimes. It is OK to ask for help, it is OK to allow yourself the privilege of guided awareness and let yourself find hope.

Life will get better with a great mentally healthy work ethic, and a good amount of **time**.

Keep up the good fight, and keep on keepin' on.

About the Author

Kevin Hines is a dedicated and hardworking advocate for mental health and suicide prevention. He has reached international audiences with his story of an unlikely survival and will to live. When Kevin was 19 years old, two years after he was diagnosed with bipolar disorder, he attempted to take his own life by jumping from the Golden Gate Bridge. He is one of thirty-three to survive the fall; however, he is the only survivor who spreads the message around the globe of living mentally well. He brings a message that *you are never alone* in this fight for wellness. Hines has reached over 350,000 people this past decade. Today, he works on legislative efforts from Patrick Kennedy's Parity Bill to local efforts to bring a barrier to the Golden Gate Bridge.

Kevin Hines's story of survival is changing and saving lives. His compelling story has touched diverse audiences on university campuses, organizations, corporations, clergy, military, clinicians, the medical community, community organizations, and international conferences. Hines believes wholeheartedly that there is light at the end of every tunnel, no matter how dark that tunnel appears to be at its beginning and that every person has the capacity to live mentally well.

Cracked, Not Broken: Surviving and Thriving After a Suicide Attempt is Hines first book. He is currently working on his second with renowned San Francisco psychiatrist Dr. Karin Hastik. Kevin lives in California with his wife and dog, happily pursuing a bright future.